UNIFICATIONISTS: WHAT THEY BELIEVE

A Glimpse at the Core Teachings of the
Unification Church

Nelson Mira

UNIFICATIONISTS: WHAT THEY BELIEVE

A Glimpse at the Core Teachings of the Unification Church

Copyright © 2015 Nelson Mira
www.discoverdp.info

ISBN - 13: 978-1502712776
ISBN - 10: 1502712776

Quotes from the *Exposition of the Divine Principle* used with permission.

Quotes from the speeches of the Reverend Sun Myung Moon used with permission.

All Scripture quotations, unless otherwise indicated, are taken from the King James Version (KJV) of the Holy Bible, a public domain in the United States, no copyright information available.

A special thanks to Mrs. Eileen Williams for her editorial assistance and encouragement.

Table of Contents

Introduction

When you hear the news of "Moonies mass wedding," where thousands of people get married at the same time in the same location and some of them meet for the very first time, what do you think? You might be thinking, "What on earth? What are these people thinking?" I am sure that those brides and bridegrooms were thinking that they made the right choice. I guess the real questions to ask are, "What compels them to do this?" and "What do they believe?"

I joined the Unification Church in 1988 and have been a follower of the late Reverend Sun Myung Moon, the church's founder, ever since. My wife and I were one of the 30,000 couples at the Unification Church's mass wedding who Reverend Moon and his wife Dr. Hak Ja Han Moon wed in Seoul, South Korea, on August 25, 1992. Father and Mother Moon matched my wife and me, and we met for the first time during that mass wedding. My wife and I are still married and happily living together and we have a wonderful daughter. Both of us are very active Unification Church members or "Unificationists"—what our church members prefer to be called—in many activities of the church in the United States, and we occasionally travel abroad to participate in our church's programs.

I spend most of my time involved with UC activities teaching the principles, or the theology, of the church. In many cases the people I encounter ask me the same questions: "Do you believe in God?" "Are you a Christian?" "Do you believe that Reverend Moon is the Messiah?" To answer such questions, there needs to be a certain amount of time to consider this since the teachings of the Unification Church are new as compared to conventional Christian

1

teachings. It is for this reason that I decided to write this book so that my readers will get at least a glimpse at the core teachings of our church.

Hopefully real understanding will temper the oft-biased articles posted on the internet and will appeal to the reader's sense of reason rather than mere emotionalism.

It is not unusual for a new religious movement to be persecuted and to be considered as a cult, especially if it is growing quickly. New movements tend to generate angst as the general population wonders about their motivation and can only imagine what the adherents actually believe. The Unification Church is not exempted from this course. The church was officially founded only in 1954, in Seoul, Korea, but it has grown to one hundred and ninety-four countries. Over the past decades, the Unification Church had been deeply misunderstood. If I were still an 'outsider' looking in, I too would have concerns if I simply listened to rumors or read the internet. If you are a sincere person who observes and analyzes various philosophies and issues according to your own conscience then this book is for you!

You may be one of those who looked at the Unification Church in a negative way, and for this reason, you are interested in this book. If that is so, I am very grateful for your decision to check this book out, and I sincerely respect your time and your opinion.

I am not writing this book to show that the Unification Church is superior to any other religion be it Mormonism or Islam or Christianity. I am writing this book to give you my understanding of how unique the basic teachings—called the "Divine Principle"—are and show you the Divine Principle's interpretations of the Bible in comparison with conventional Christian interpretations. I believe the Divine Principle clarifies and adds much to current interpretations.

I will be quoting from *Exposition of the Divine Principle* (1996), and from here on I will simply call it *the Divine Principle.* Most of what you will read are my own commentaries. The Bible quotes I use to augment our discussion are excerpted from the King James Version. I will also include several speeches by Reverend Sun Myung Moon.

Perhaps you are interested to know about the Unification Church's mass wedding, and for that, I have included an entire chapter explaining its uniqueness.

Some Unificationists may disagree with me for arguing the point that the Divine Principle is different from conventional Christian teachings. However, UC followers while recognizing that our teachings are unique, often discourage debate with the understanding that God guides *all* religions to accomplish His will and His desire to bring mankind back into an ideal world of harmony. Thus our approach by the very definition of our teaching is ecumenical or interfaith. My book is not about posing a debate—instead this is my attempt to explain the Divine Principle concisely and to perhaps set the record straight on points of confusion.

There are so many profound similarities between our teachings and the teachings from all the major religions. Reverend Moon himself mentioned in one of his speeches that seventy percent of our teachings are similar to other religions. I totally agree, and believe that the goal of every religion is to establish peace and harmony on earth through love and forgiveness. The goals are the same; the practices are different.

The deepest contents of the Divine Principle reveal the heart of God. To understand the Principles fully on an intellectual level one should attend a minimum of two days of lectures which are usually given workshop style and are open to anyone. When I joined the Unification Church, I attended a twenty-one-day workshop on the Divine Principle to grasp its entire contents. I have spent most of my time with the church teaching the Divine Principle, and yet I feel that I still need to understand more about its deepest aspects. The Divine Principle is not only a teaching—it's a way of life. To understand the essence of the Divine Principle and the heart of God, deep prayer and reflection is also needed. Reverend and Mrs. Sun Myung Moon published thousands of volumes of their speeches explaining God and humanity related to the teachings of the Divine Principle.

The thirteen chapters of the *Exposition of the Divine Principle* can be grouped into three major parts: "Principles of Creation," which explains the ideal that comes from God and which humanity is striving to reach (consciously or not); "The Fall," which explains why this ideal has not been realized; and "Restoration," which explains how God works throughout history to restore this ideal. As you can see, the Divine Principle is not about arguing how superior it is compared with conventional teachings, but its purpose is to reveal God's intention for us, His children, and demonstrate - in detail - how He labored with anguish throughout human history to bring mankind out of the dungeons of despair.

Let's get to what you want to know the most. You have probably heard, read, and even scorned the idea that Unificationists claim that the Reverend Sun Myung Moon is the Second Coming of Christ. "Is he the Messiah?" you ask. My answer is both "yes" and "no." It all depends on how you define the words "Messiah" and "Christ." If you believe the literal interpretation of the Bible that the Messiah will come from the clouds surrounded by platoons of angels blowing their trumpets and the dead will rise from their graves, then Reverend Moon is definitely not the one. However, if you believe that Christ's return, will mostly likely NOT be a fantastical event that defies scientific logic, but instead could be a real-life person and a real-life movement with Jesus' same mission then it makes sense that the Second Coming of Christ is upon us. If one is observant there are many apparent signs that were prophesied in the Bible. I will discuss this topic later because I am going to place more emphasis on the nature of Jesus and his mission and why his work needs fulfillment still.

If you are curious about the Unification Church's mass wedding, this book is for you. I wrote an entire chapter explaining this event and what is behind it.

Let's first look at the different Bible interpretations of the Divine Principle as compared to the conventional Christian interpretations.

Not Everything is Printed in the Bible

This doesn't make any sense, of course, because not everything can be printed in the Bible, but to fundamentalists, any religious teachings that are not literally interpreted word for word are considered *heresy*—"a belief or opinion that does not agree with the official belief or opinion of a particular religion" (*Merriam-Webster.com.*1 July 2014). Unificationists believe that not all of God's messages were printed in the Bible. Why, then, is it that many Christians believe there is no other revelation outside of the Bible?

Christians believe that Jesus Christ fulfilled everything he needed to accomplish, including bringing the words of God to the earth.

> "Think not that I am come to destroy the law, or the prophets: I am not come to destroy, but to fulfill." (Matthew 5:17)

From this understanding, the Bible is complete, finished, a done deal. What does the Divine Principle say about this? The Divine Principle tells us that God will and has revealed more insight and wisdom that is not written in the Bible. In this sense, the Bible is *not* complete. If human history is evolving towards an ideal why would revelation just stop during one particular era? God is a living God and His word is ever being expressed through humankind especially through those spiritually attuned.

It is written in the Bible that the first human ancestors, Adam and Eve disobeyed God's commandment, which was not to eat the fruit of the Tree of the Knowledge of Good and Evil. We will refer to this event as the "Fall." If they fulfilled God's commandment, they would have reflected God's character and perfection. God would have been able to relate to them directly. Unfortunately, because of the Fall, our first ancestors' ability to relate with God was severed because their spiritual state and intellectual level fell to a very low state. This state was passed on to their descendants to this day

At every stage in human history, God is actively working to bring humanity back to a *fulfilled* state from a *fallen* state. However, He can only relate to His children according to each person's own spiritual maturity.

Through the process of God's work to bring back humanity to His side, the spirituality and intellect of fallen people have gradually developed. As our spiritual and intellectual levels have grown during each age, God has been able to revise His approach to us. Approximately four thousand years ago in Abraham's time when the people's spirituality and intellect were extremely low, God had to have them relate to Him through the offering of sacrifices. They were even too immature to respond to laws and commandments, so God had the people of that time offer the finest fruits of their labor such as food and animals.

Several hundred years later at the time of Moses, people's spiritual and intellectual state gradually developed to a higher level, so God carried out the dispensation through laws—such as the "Ten Commandments." When Jesus came, instead of repeating the same dispensation through laws or commandments, God worked in a new way to bring people closer to Him by giving the Gospel at a level appropriate for the spirituality and intellect of the people of that age. The new gospel even transcended the law; it was about love.

However, the chosen people, who so devoutly believed in God, did not recognize His son, Jesus, as the one they were waiting for. Why were they unable to recognize him? At that time, the chosen people revered and upheld the laws that Moses installed which for most of them was the only way to follow God. But, then God began to approach the chosen people through Jesus himself by means of the new dispensation of the Gospel, an expression of God's will different from what they already learned and practiced. Therefore, the chosen people failed to accept Jesus as the Messiah whom God sent. They were stuck in the old way of thinking.

The really good news is that today a new revelation from God is imminent. As humanity's spirituality and intellect develop, God has always adopted a corresponding method to reach His children. We need to understand that the present focus of God's dispensation is not the people of Jesus' time two thousand years ago. The present focus is on the contemporary person, you and me, living here and now.

This diagram below shows God's way of relating to humanity at each stage in history:

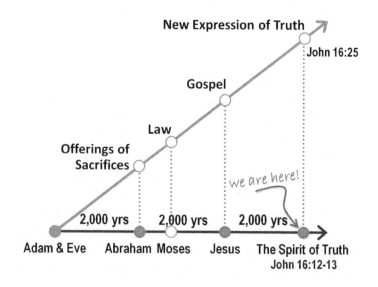

We need a new expression of truth from God now! Most people today have lost interest in and are turning away from the church. The rational and scientific emphasis of people demands a clearer and deeper understanding of the Bible. There is also a demand for practical explanations of the seeming contradictions in many religious teachings and practices before people will take up a religious way of life. Humanity needs a new, deeper expression of truth from God. World religions are failing to lead the modern age toward a harmonious world. Violence, war, racism, terrorism, and the unequal distribution of wealth are prevalent. We are witnessing the rapid collapse of modern civilizations and of order in society with no satisfactory solution in sight. Confusion throughout society about standards of value and conduct has resulted in a strong trend toward the breakdown of the family and increased immorality. None of these crises has been completely eradicated since the beginning of time. Thus, a concordant solution - a shift - is needed. Since God is alive, He will definitely save humankind from these turbulent times through a new and revolutionary approach. We are living in a new and exciting age!

Another reason why a new expression of truth is imperative is because of the need to unite science and religion. Today, we see many arguments between scientific leaning people and religious people as to whether there is a spiritual realm or not. The Divine Principle explains that spiritual knowledge alone is not enough, nor is science enough. We need both explanations to understand the universe in its totality.

We read in the Bible that God is alive and working in accordance to the level of spirituality of fallen people, so we can know that God will definitely give humanity a new expression of truth, one that can lead the people of this age to discover God anew and establish His Kingdom on Earth - not just in some fairytale heaven.

Many difficult conundrums arise when one examines the Bible. This is because answers to many questions have been told in parables and symbols and have yet to be clearly explained. Jesus said, "These things have I spoken unto you in proverbs: but the time cometh, when I shall no more speak unto you in proverbs, but I shall shew you plainly of the Father" (John 16:25). Jesus also said, "I have yet many things to say unto you, but ye cannot bear them now. Howbeit when he, the Spirit of truth, is come, he will guide you into all truth: for he shall not speak of himself; but whatsoever he shall hear, that shall he speak: and he will shew you things to come" (John 16:12-13). Both of these passages indicates that in the "Last Days," a new expression of the truth will be revealed to humanity.

When the new revelation comes, there will be many aspects that may not be understood in light of conventional doctrine or tradition. When Jesus brought the Gospel, the people of his time were bound to such a literal interpretation of the Old Testament that they could not understand Him. Jesus was branded as a heretic, which led Him to His crucifixion. It was for this reason that Jesus said, "And no man putteth new wine into old bottles: else the new wine doth burst the bottles, and the wine is spilled, and the bottles will be marred: but new wine must be put into new bottles" (Mark 2:22). He was teaching them that they had to make their hearts and minds new to receive the new expression of truth.

Unificationists claim that the Divine Principle, and the speeches of the Reverend and Mrs. Sun Myung Moon, are this new expression of truth needed for the times we live in:

At age fifteen, while deep in prayer he had a vision of Jesus Christ who called him to dedicate his life to God and the salvation of humankind. Despite his youth and the seeming impossibility of the mission, he accepted God's call. But he knew he could not succeed in his task without a profound understanding of the Creator, His creation and His plan for man. He intensified his quest for the truth, spending days and nights in passionate prayer, rigorous fasting, and study. His method was to posit specific questions, research answers in the physical and spiritual worlds, and then seek confirmation for those answers through prayer. On several occasions, he was guided directly by Abraham, Moses, Jesus, Mohammed, Buddha and other saints and sages of all faiths, who met him in spirit and contributed to his understanding of God and the complex history of God's relationship with humankind. By the age of 25, he had developed the fundamentals of his teaching, the Divine Principle.

(www.ReverendSunMyungMoon.org, 1 July 2014)

In every corner of the world, countless souls who had been groping in the darkness are receiving the light of this new truth and are being reborn. As we witness this, we cannot stop shedding tears of deepest inspiration. We desire from the bottom of our hearts that its light quickly fills the earth. (*Exposition of the Divine Principle,* 12)

God Did Not Create the Universe Within a Literal Six-Day Period

According to the conventional belief, God created the universe in only six literal days. Here's what the Bible says in Genesis, chapter 1:

1   In the beginning God created the heaven and the earth.

2   And the earth was without form, and void; and darkness was upon the face of the deep. And the Spirit of God moved upon the face of the waters.

3   And God said, Let there be light: and there was light.

4   And God saw the light, that it was good: and God divided the light from the darkness.

5   And God called the light Day, and the darkness he called Night. And the evening and the morning were the **first day**.

6   And God said, Let there be a firmament in the midst of the waters, and let it divide the waters from the waters.

7   And God made the firmament, and divided the waters which were under the firmament from the waters which were above the firmament: and it was so.

8   And God called the firmament Heaven. And the evening and the morning were the **second day**.

9   And God said, Let the waters under the heaven be gathered together unto one place, and let the dry land appear: and it was so.

10 And God called the dry land Earth; and the gathering together of the waters called he Seas: and God saw that it was good.

11 And God said, Let the earth bring forth grass, the herb yielding seed, and the fruit tree yielding fruit after his kind, whose seed is in itself, upon the earth: and it was so.

12 And the earth brought forth grass, and herb yielding seed after his kind, and the tree yielding fruit, whose seed was in itself, after his kind: and God saw that it was good.

13 And the evening and the morning were the **third day**.

14 And God said, Let there be lights in the firmament of the heaven to divide the day from the night; and let them be for signs, and for seasons, and for days, and years:

15 And let them be for lights in the firmament of the heaven to give light upon the earth: and it was so.

16 And God made two great lights; the greater light to rule the day, and the lesser light to rule the night: he made the stars also.

17 And God set them in the firmament of the heaven to give light upon the earth,

18 And to rule over the day and over the night, and to divide the light from the darkness: and God saw that it was good.

19 And the evening and the morning were the **fourth day**.

20 And God said, Let the waters bring forth abundantly the moving creature that hath life, and fowl that may fly above the earth in the open firmament of heaven.

21 And God created great whales, and every living creature that moveth, which the waters brought forth abundantly, after their kind, and every winged fowl after his kind: and God saw that it was good.

22 And God blessed them, saying, Be fruitful, and multiply, and fill the waters in the seas, and let fowl multiply in the earth.

23 And the evening and the morning were the **fifth day**.

24 And God said, Let the earth bring forth the living creature after his kind, cattle, and creeping thing, and beast of the earth after his kind: and it was so.

25 And God made the beast of the earth after his kind, and cattle after their kind, and every thing that creepeth upon the earth after his kind: and God saw that it was good.

26 And God said, Let us make man in our image, after our likeness: and let them have dominion over the fish of the sea, and over the fowl of the air, and over the cattle, and over all the earth, and over every creeping thing that creepeth upon the earth.

27 So God created man in his own image, in the image of God created he him; male and female created he them.

28 And God blessed them, and God said unto them, Be fruitful, and multiply, and replenish the earth, and subdue it: and have dominion over the fish of the sea, and over the fowl of the air, and over every living thing that moveth upon the earth.

29 And God said, Behold, I have given you every herb bearing seed, which is upon the face of all the earth, and every tree, in the which is the fruit of a tree yielding seed; to you it shall be for meat.

30 And to every beast of the earth, and to every fowl of the air, and to every thing that creepeth upon the earth, wherein there is life, I have given every green herb for meat: and it was so.

31 And God saw every thing that he had made, and, behold, it was very good. And the evening and the morning were the **sixth day**.

And in Genesis 2:2, we read, "And on the seventh day God ended his work which he had made; and he rested on the **seventh day** from all his work which he had made."

Some Christians believe that the earth is only about six thousand years old. This is because if we examine the Bible, we find out that Adam and Eve, the biblical first man and woman whom God created on the seventh day, lived approximately around 4000 BC. This understanding is completely inconsistent with scientific studies and facts.

The Divine Principle reconciles this contradiction between religion and science by explaining that the seven days of creation in the Bible are symbolic. The days mentioned in Genesis 1 are not twenty-four-hour periods. Where can we find a supporting verse from the Bible? It is in 2 Peter 3:8: "But, beloved, be not ignorant of this one thing, that one day is with the Lord as a thousand years, and a thousand years as one day."

Then, what does it mean when the Bible says that the earth was created in seven days? Those days represent the creation's periods of time, which lasted thousands of years.

The Divine Principle states:

> The process of creation recorded in the Bible bears some resemblance to the theory of the origin and formation of the universe as described by modern science. According to modern science, the universe began as expanding plasma. Out of the chaos and void of space, the heavenly bodies formed and gave light. As the molten earth cooled, volcanic eruptions filled the sky with a firmament of water. The land rose and the

water fell as rain, creating the continents and oceans. Next, the lower plants and animals came into being. Then came fish, birds, mammals, and finally humankind, in that order. The age of the earth is calculated to be several billion years. Considering that the account of the creation of the universe recorded in the Bible thousands of years ago nearly coincides with the findings of modern scientific research, we are reassured that this biblical record must be a revelation from God.

The universe did not suddenly spring forth complete, without regard to the flow of time. In fact, its origin and development took an enormous length of time. Therefore, the biblical period of six days for the completion of the universe is not to be reckoned by the number of literal sunrises and sunsets. It symbolizes six ordered periods in the creation process. (*Exposition of the Divine Principle,* 40)

The Divine Principle explains that those six days of creation are not literal twenty-four-hour days. Each day of creation consisted of millions of years. In one of Reverend Moon's speeches, he said that even in creating a single tiny flower, God invested His whole heart and energy. Then, how much more did God invest His time and heart in creating humankind and the universe? We imagine it would be more than that. He did not create the universe by snapping his fingers or in the blink of His eyes. The entire creation itself has amazing value because God puts His whole heart and energy into the process of creating. Each and every creature in the universe is very precious to God and has unique value.

Father and Mother God - Dual Characteristics

In most religions, particularly with Christianity, God has been referred to solely as an almighty masculine being. When we read the Bible, we see that the God of Noah, Abraham, and Moses is a masculine being. Jesus also called God the father, "Our Father in heaven ..." (Matthew 6:9), signifying that God is a masculine God. Therefore, God is referred to as the Heavenly Father.

Additionally, the Divine Principle explains that God has the "dual characteristics" of masculinity and femininity, or "yang" and "yin" as defined in Chinese philosophy. God's image is male *and* female. We find this in the Bible:

> So God created man in his own image, in the image of God created he him; male and female created he them. (Genesis 1:27)

This verse signifies that although God is a masculine being, an aspect of 'Him' is also feminine. Therefore, we can say that God is our Heavenly Father as well as our Heavenly Mother. He is one God but capable of loving his children with fatherly and motherly love as our Heavenly Parent. This means that humanity experiences parental love from a God who is both father and mother. In the Unification Church we refer to God as our Heavenly Parent - the source of all parental love which is ultimately expressed through humans themselves in loving their own children.

We observe the pattern of dual characteristics throughout all of nature. The Divine Principle goes further to explain the concept of the yang and yin characteristics of God.

All things reflect God's nature; therefore, everything in the universe is composed of dual characteristics. Yang and yin must engage in harmonious, giving and receiving reciprocal relationships to maintain their existence and to reproduce. Subatomic particles, the basic building blocks of all matter, for example, possess a positive charge and a negative charge. When these charges combine through the reciprocal relationship of their dual characteristics, they form an atom. When the dual characteristics within one atom enter into reciprocal relationships with those in another atom, they form a molecule. Molecules formed in this manner engage in further reciprocal relationships between their dual characteristics eventually to become nourishment fit for consumption by plants and animals. Plants propagate by means of their stamens and pistils. Animals multiply and maintain their species through the relationship between males and females. Likewise, human beings multiply and maintain their species through the relationship between a man and a woman.

In human beings, God's harmonious dual characteristics are manifested separately as man and woman (Genesis 1:27). In order to resemble God, both man and woman must become as one. Hence, in the Bible it says:

> For this cause shall a man leave his father and mother, and shall be joined unto his wife, and they two shall be one flesh. (Ephesians 5:31)

Reverend Sun Myung Moon said:

> *God is the harmonious union of the dual characteristics of masculinity and femininity. Creation occurs by the principle that God's internal nature divides into two separate characteristics, which then re-unite in a form*

that resembles God's original internal nature. Man and woman are born each resembling one of God's characteristics. That is, the union of God's son and God's daughter is the union of God's masculinity and God's femininity. In their harmonious union they resemble God. For this reason, husband and wife are a unified body that represents God in His entirety. (April 16, 1960)

Woman has a feminine nature and man has a masculine nature; God made them as divided embodiments of Himself. How can they come together as one? Through love. Having formerly been divided, when they come together they will experience how strong the love is that God had been holding within Himself. Otherwise, they would never know God's love. (January 8, 1989)

God created human beings as male and female in His image. Therefore, it is only when a man and a woman become one that they come to resemble God. Husband and wife are a unified body that represent God in His entirety. God's immeasurable love can be experienced through a perfect union between a man and a woman because this state of oneness manifests God's characteristics, allowing God to dwell in them. The beauty of this union was meant to last for eternity.

The Origin of 'Sin': The Serpent, Hell, and Adam and Eve - Literal *or* Not?

"Original sin"—what an infamous phrase! This is the root cause of all the evils in the world, at least for Christians. No matter what you do, part of you is evil because you have the original sin. What is it? Well, the simple explanation according to Wikipedia is:

> Original sin, also called ancestral sin, is the Christian doctrine of humanity's state of sin resulting from the fall of man, stemming from Adam's rebellion in Eden. This condition has been characterized in many ways, ranging from something as insignificant as a slight deficiency, or a tendency toward sin yet without collective guilt, referred to as a "sin nature," to something as drastic as total depravity or automatic guilt of all humans through collective guilt. (Wikipedia.com, 1 July 2014)

Catholics and Protestants alike believe that we are all born sinners. Hence, Martin Luther (1483–1546) asserted that human beings inherit Adamic guilt and are in a state of sin from the moment of conception.

Our first human ancestors, Adam and Eve, committed this very first sin in the Garden of Eden. What the heck happened in the Garden of Eden anyway? The Bible says that God gave a commandment to Adam and Eve **not to eat the forbidden fruit of the Tree of Knowledge of Good and Evil, for the day that they ate of it, they would surely die** (Genesis 2:17). However, the serpent tempted Eve and she ate the fruit and shared it to Adam. This was the

20

"Fall." As a result, Adam and Eve were chased out from the Garden of Eden, and from then on, sorrows came to exist and were inherited by all of their descendants until to this very day.

Christians have held to a vague belief that Adam and Eve's eating the fruit of the Tree of Knowledge of Good and Evil was the root of sin, *the original sin.*

What was the Forbidden Fruit?

Many Christians believe that the fruit of the Tree of Knowledge of Good and Evil was a fruit of an actual tree, some say even that it was an apple. The Divine Principle teaches that again this imagery is symbolic. We may ask, "How, then, can a food which one eats cause one to commit sin?" There are those who believe that God gave the commandment to Adam and Eve not to eat the fruit in order to test their obedience to Him. The Divine Principle claims that it was not a test. Would the God of love test His children so mercilessly by a means that could cause their death? Would God, the loving Parent of humanity, make a fruit which could cause the Fall to look so attractive and place it where His children could reach it so easily? Surely, that would be a psychopathic God by any definition. Adam and Eve knew they would commit a horrible mistake the moment they ate the fruit, for God had told them so. Yet still they ate it. They did not lack for food. They would not have risked their lives and disobeyed God only to obtain some delicacy.

What was the forbidden 'fruit'? The fruit of the Tree of the Knowledge of Good and Evil could not have been an ordinary fruit. It must have been something so extraordinarily stimulating that even the fear of death did not deter them

21

from grasping it. The fruit was not a material fruit. It must have been a symbol that represented something else.

The forbidden fruit symbolizes **immature sexual love.** Adam and Eve succumbed to the temptation of the serpent to engage in fornication before they were spiritually mature and blessed by God in marriage.

Evidence of this sexual act was the manner in which their guilt was expressed. Adam and Eve covered their sexual parts after they ate the fruit because they were ashamed of their nakedness. We can read in Genesis 3:6-10:

> And when the woman saw that the tree was good for food, and that it was pleasant to the eyes, and a tree to be desired to make one wise, she took of the fruit thereof, and did eat, and gave also unto her husband with her; and he did eat. And the eyes of them both were opened, and they knew that they were naked; and they sewed fig leaves together, and made themselves aprons. And they heard the voice of the Lord God walking in the garden in the cool of the day: and Adam and his wife hid themselves from the presence of the Lord God amongst the trees of the garden. And the Lord God called unto Adam, and said unto him, Where art thou? And he said, I heard thy voice in the garden, and I was afraid, because I was naked; and I hid myself.

The Divine Principle says:

> We read that before they fell, Adam and Eve were both naked, and were not ashamed. After the Fall, however, they felt ashamed of their nakedness and sewed fig leaves together into aprons to cover their lower parts. If they had committed a crime by eating

some actual fruit from a tree called the tree of the knowledge of good and evil, then they certainly would have covered their hands or mouths instead. It is human nature to conceal one's faults. Thus, the act of covering their lower parts shows that these parts, and not their mouths, were the source of their shame. In Job 31:33, it is written, "If I have concealed my transgressions like Adam, by hiding my iniquity in my bosom." (*Exposition of the Divine Principle,* 59)

If we look at the serious consequences of the Fall, it really makes sense that the sin was an illicit sexual relationship. Because of their illicit act, Adam and Eve bound themselves in blood ties with the fallen archangel Lucifer and inherited the devil's fallen lineage rather than God's. This is why Jesus said, "You are of your father the devil" (John 8:44) and called them a "generation of vipers" (Matthew 3:7, 12:34, 23:33 and Luke 3:7). St. Paul wrote, "Not only the creation, but we ourselves, who have the first fruits of the Spirit, groan inwardly as we wait for adoption as sons" (Romans 8:23), indicating that no one belongs to the lineage of God. Due to the Fall of the first human ancestors, human beings are of the lineage of Satan. The Bible uses fruit as the symbol because fruit bears seeds. It is through the seeds that more fruit is reproduced. In a very real sense human beings have been the product of a 'bad seed' the fallen Adam and Eve rather than the product of 'good seed' - or of a Godly union between Adam and Eve.

Sometimes when I explain this concept to certain Christian friends, they laugh at it. However, becoming the children of Lucifer simply by eating an apple, banana, or whatever fruit people refer to, does not make sense. Inheriting a blood lineage suggests a sexual relationship. Eating a literal fruit certainly would not result in the disastrous legacy of inheriting a fallen state - separated from our God, our true nature and even one another.

However, the greatest consequence of the Fall was that God lost His beloved children. He agonized over this loss to the extent that He was sorry He created human beings: "And it repented the Lord that he had made man on the earth, and it grieved him at his heart" (Genesis 6:6). Thus, God had walked a painful path of dispensation to redeem His children.

It says in the Bible that Adam and Eve continued to live for many years after they disobeyed God. They did not die physically right after they ate the fruit, but their lineage from God was cut off, and this is what the Bible considers as their death: "... for in the day that thou eatest thereof thou shalt surely die" (Genesis 2:17). 'Death' meaning the loss of their spiritual lives and not their literal physical death.

The Serpent was Not a Literal Snake

There were three players involved in the process of the Fall in the Garden of Eden. The *Tree of Life*, the *Tree of Knowledge of Good and Evil*, and the *Serpent*. According to the Divine Principle, the Tree of Life symbolized Adam, while the Tree of the Knowledge of Good and Evil symbolized Eve.

However, let's talk about this serpent since he seems to be the cause of so much trouble! There are those who believe that the serpent was an actual snake. If that were the case, it would have been impossible for the serpent to tempt Eve because snakes don't talk and don't know God's will. The Divine Principle says that it symbolized another being in the garden—the archangel *Lucifer.*

24

God Did Not Create Evil or Hell

The very fact of the existence of evil on the one hand causes doubt about the existence of God on the other. If there is a just and loving God, why does He allow evil? This is an important question. While there is a strong debate whether God originated evil or not, the Divine Principle strongly argues that the origin of evil does not come from God.

The Divine Principle explains that God created His entire creation only to be good. In Genesis 1:31 we read that God rejoiced because everything He had created was 'very good'. However, due to the Fall, God grieved for the loss of His children (Genesis 6:6). This tells us that God did not intend for evil to exist in this world. It was because of the Fall that the Archangel, Lucifer, became Satan and acted as the ruler of the world (John 12:31, 2 Corinthians 4:4). Lucifer's fall from grace is the starting point of evil - which was then substantiated - and multiplied - through Adam and Eve and their descendents.

These days there are many examples in both Christian sermons and in the Bible that seem to support the idea that God is a tyrannical ruthless judge who acts capriciously to punish man. However, the holder of most influence, Satan came to 'rule the world' because of the Fall, and became the god of evil, contrary to God's nature of goodness. It is very important to realize that every misfortune that has come to this world is the work of Satan and fallen man - not of God. God has been working to eliminate evil once and for all.

Adam, Eve, and the Angels Were Not Created Perfect

If God is perfect, then how would it be possible for Adam and Eve to commit sin? There is a common misunderstanding that when God created Adam, Eve, and the Archangel, they were already in their perfect state, perfect in character and deed. With this understanding some Christians argue that it was God's will that the Fall occurred. The Divine Principle says that they were not perfect, but instead they were *growing toward maturity* when the Fall occurred. Every creature from plants to man goes through this process of growth. Reverend Moon's comment on this is:

> *We should not think that when God created Adam and Eve from clay, He created them as adults. Rather, God created them as infants. God went through the same process as a mother who gives birth to her baby, cradles them, and raises them. (January 20, 1992)*

During their growing period, when Adam and Eve were still immature growing up to become husband and wife, God knew that they could make mistakes. This was the reason why God gave them the commandment not to 'eat the fruit', meaning not to have sex, because they were simply not mature enough.

Knowing that God gave them the commandment to wait means that Adam and Eve were not yet perfect. The commandment was their responsibility to keep. The Divine Principle explains why the commandment was necessary:

> In their immature state, God could not directly govern Adam and Eve through love. Because the pow-

er of love is stronger than the power of the Principle, God foresaw that if they ever formed a common base with the Archangel, there was a possibility that they could succumb to the power of unprincipled love and fall. To prevent this, God gave Adam and Eve the commandment that forbade them from relating with the Archangel in this way. No matter how powerful the unprincipled love of the Archangel might be, had Adam and Eve adhered to God's commandment, forming a common base with God and engaging in give and take with Him and no other, the power of the Archangel's unprincipled love would not have affected them and they would never have fallen. Tragically, Adam and Eve did not obey the commandment, but formed a common base with the Archangel and had give and take with him. Hence, the power of illicit love pushed them off the track. (*Exposition of the Divine Principle*, 66-67)

God endowed Adam and Eve with freedom and with the responsibility to reach their own individual perfection, by following His commandment and fulfilling their own portion of responsibility.

Another reason why God had them follow the commandment:

It was not only to prevent their fall that God gave immature human beings the commandment. God also wanted them to enjoy dominion over the natural world including the angels-by inheriting His creative nature. In order to inherit this creatorship, human beings should perfect themselves through their faith in the Word as their own portion of responsibility.

God gave the commandment not to the Archangel but only to the human beings. God wished to exalt the dignity of human beings as bestowed by the Principle of Creation, which entitled them to stand as God's children and govern even the angels. (*Exposition of the Divine Principle,* 67)

Consequently, God did not create His children to be like machines or robots. He gave them freedom and responsibility which set them apart from other creatures. This responsibility was a great opportunity for human beings to be qualified as the co-creators of God. If Adam and Eve would have achieved perfection and become one with God, they would have had the right to 'eat the fruit' and establish a family, society, nation, and eventually a world where only goodness dwelled.

What about the state of the Archangel? The Divine Principle says that the Archangel Lucifer would have achieved perfection as well if he fulfilled his tasks to guide Adam and Eve to reach perfection themselves.

The Fall was a tragedy and it caused unfathomable pain and sorrow to God and to humanity. Some people claim that this proves that God made a mistake or that God is fallible. This is contrary to what we know about God's perfection, as Jesus said, "Be ye therefore perfect, even as your Father which is in heaven is perfect." (Matthew 5:48). The Divine Principle says that God did not make a mistake rather the fulfillment of God's plan rests in humanity's hands. It says in Genesis that Adam turned and blamed Eve and in turn she blamed Lucifer. It seems that mankind has been blaming God ever since.

The End of Times

Concerning "eschatology," or the doctrine of the Last Days, many Christians believe literally what is written in the Bible:

> Looking for and hastening unto the coming of the day of God, wherein the heavens being on fire shall be dissolved, and the elements shall melt with fervent heat? (2 Peter 3:12)

> Immediately after the tribulation of those days shall the sun be darkened, and the moon shall not give her light, and the stars shall fall from heaven, and the powers of the heavens shall be shaken ... (Matthew 24:29)

> For the Lord himself shall descend from heaven with a shout, with the voice of the archangel, and with the trumpet of God: and the dead in Christ shall rise first: Then we which are alive and remain shall be caught up together with them in the clouds, to meet the Lord in the air: and so shall we ever be with the Lord. (1 Thessalonians 4:16-17)

Sounds very chaotic, doesn't it? The description of the Last Days sounds like the total destruction of the earth as portrayed in the blockbuster movies *2012* or *Armageddon*. A big question is whether these events will take place literally or whether the verses are symbolic, as we have already noted, are many parts of the Bible.

Here are some literal interpretations of conven-tional Christian doctrines about the Last Days:

1. The Last Days is the end of the world.
2. Heaven and earth will be destroyed, and a new heaven and new earth will be created.
3. Heaven and earth will be judged by fire.
4. The dead will rise from their tombs.
5. People on earth will be caught up to meet the Lord in the air.
6. The sun will darken, the moon will not give light, and the stars will fall from heaven.

The Divine Principle says that the six above interpretations are not literal but symbolic. Here are the Divine Principle's interpretations:

1. The Last Days is the end of the world.

It was written that God determined to destroy the earth in Noah's time:

> The earth also was corrupt before God, and the earth was filled with violence. And God looked upon the earth, and, behold, it was corrupt; for all flesh had corrupted his way upon the earth. And God said unto Noah, The end of all flesh is come before me; for the earth is filled with violence through them; and, behold, I will destroy them with the earth. (Genesis 6:11-13)

From this verse, we can say that Noah's time was the Last Days, yet the earth was not destroyed.

God created the earth to last forever: "And he built his sanctuary like high palaces, like the earth which he hath established forever" (Psalm 78:69). The earth is the object partner of God. God, the subject partner, is eternal; likewise, earth should also be eternal. An Almighty God would never be pleased with having created a world so fragile that it could perish.

The goal of salvation is the restoration of what was lost in the Garden of Eden. If the world is going to end literally, then everything will perish and every human being would die and God's desire on earth will not be realized. As God said in Isaiah 46:11, **"I have spoken it, I will also bring it to pass; I have purposed it, I will also do it."** Ecclesiastes 1:4 tells us that God will never abandon His purpose: "One generation passeth away, and another generation cometh: but the earth abideth forever." God's desire is to build the Kingdom of Heaven on this earth, not somewhere else or on some other planet. The world that we are living in is the place where Adam and Eve lived and where God meant to establish His eternal kingdom. When our bodies return to dust, "For dust thou art, and unto dust shalt thou return" (Genesis 3:19), our spirit enters God's kingdom in the spiritual realm.

2. Heaven and earth will be destroyed, and a new heaven and new earth will be created.

Earth will not be destroyed, but evil sovereignties will end, and a new sovereignty will reign. What then is the meaning of the prophecies of the earth's destruction in the Last Days? For instance:

> Looking for and hasting unto the coming of the day of God, wherein the heavens being on fire shall be dissolved, and the elements shall melt with fervent heat? Nevertheless we, according to his promise, look for new heavens and a new earth, wherein dwelleth righteousness. (2 Peter 3:12-13)

31

> And I saw a new heaven and a new earth: for the first heaven and the first earth were passed away; and there was no more sea. (Revelation 21:1)

From our understanding of history we know that to destroy a nation is to overthrow its sovereignty. To erect a new nation is to establish a new sovereignty. Therefore, the prophecies that heaven and earth will be destroyed mean that the tyranny of Satan will be overthrown. The emergence of a new heaven and new earth signifies the establishment of the kingdom of heaven in the spirit world and on earth under God's sovereignty founded on Christ.

3. Heaven and earth will be judged by fire.

Jesus came into the world to cast judgment, for he said, "For judgment I am come into this world" (John 9:39). "I am come to send fire on the earth; and what will I, if it be already kindled?" (Luke 12:49). "Fire" here represents the means of the judgment for which Jesus came into the world. However, there is no record in the Bible that in his time Jesus judged the world with literal fire. Therefore, the verses referring to fire must be symbolic.

Judgment by fire represents judgment by the Word of God. Jesus said, "Is not my word like as a fire? saith the Lord; and like a hammer that breaketh the rock in pieces?" (Jeremiah 23:29).

4. The dead will rise from their tombs.

It is written in the Bible that in the Last Days the dead will rise from their graves:

> For the Lord himself shall descend from heaven with a shout, with the voice of the archangel, and with the

trumpet of God: and the dead in Christ shall rise first. (1 Thessalonians 4:16)

This verse is symbolic as well. Those dead bodies had long been decomposed, and it would be impossible for them to rise literally with their own flesh from their graves! Our physical bodies are meant to return to dust in this physical world when we die, while our spirit is meant to live eternally in the spirit world. The Bible says, "Then shall the dust return to the earth as it was: and the spirit shall return unto God who gave it" (Ecclesiastes 12:7).

There was a similar event when the dead rose from their tombs at the time of Jesus' death:

> And the graves were opened; and many bodies of the saints which slept arose, And came out of the graves after his resurrection, and went into the holy city, and appeared unto many. (Matthew 27:52-53)

These verses are also meant to be symbolic. If the saints really had risen from their tombs in the flesh, then surely their deeds would have been recorded in the Bible. However, we find no such records. If the physical bodies of the saints of the Old Testament Age had actually risen from their tombs and appeared before many people in Jerusalem, they would certainly have testified to the people about Jesus as the Messiah. After hearing such testimony, Jesus' followers would have been accepted without persecution. However, we know that Jesus' twelve disciples were scattered and persecuted after Jesus' crucifixion.

What does the Bible mean when it says that the bodies of the saints rose from their tombs? The people who witnessed the incidents of the saints rising from their tombs were people possessing keen spiritual awareness who could perceive the spirit bodies of the past saints being resurrected spiritually and appearing in Jerusalem. What does "the tomb" symbolize? It symbolizes the region of the spirit world where the spirits of the Old Testament saints were abiding. This realm of the spirit world appeared to be a dark place. Hence, it was referred to as a tomb, but after Jesus' victory on the cross, this spiritual realm was opened and the high spirits could ascend to Paradise with Jesus.

5. People on earth will be caught up to meet the Lord in the air.

Again, the Divine Principle says that this is symbolic. Those dead people's bodies are already decomposed. Living beings lifted up to meet the Lord in the clouds would not make any sense either. If we all were lifted up into the clouds in the flesh, where would we dwell? On a humorous note - a Unificationist friend of mine said to me that indeed Christ had returned to earth through the cloud, but by "cloud" he meant the Internet - a place where the Lord of the Second Advent can be heard about in every corner of the world at the same time.

I'm sure you've heard the word, "rapture." Wikipedia defines it as "a term in Christian eschatology which refers to 'being caught up' as discussed in 1 Thessalonians 4:17, when the 'dead in Christ' and 'we who are alive and remain' will be 'caught up in the clouds' to meet 'the Lord in the air'" (Wikipedia.com, 2 July 2014).

If we examine this definition of rapture, it is easy to take the verses literally. Once again the meaning of these verses are symbolic. Here's what the Divine Principle says:

> The "air" mentioned in this verse does not refer to the sky over our heads. In the Bible, "earth" is often a

symbol for the fallen world under the sway of evil sovereignty, while "Heaven" is often a symbol for the sinless world of good sovereignty. The omnipresent God certainly dwells everywhere on the earth, yet we pray, "Our Father who art in heaven." (Matthew 6:9) Even though Jesus was born on the earth, he is referred to as "he who descended from Heaven, the Son of man." (John 3:13) Meeting the Lord in the air means that the saints will receive the Lord in the world of good sovereignty when Christ comes again and restore the Kingdom of Heaven on earth by defeating the kingdom of Satan. (*Exposition of the Divine Principle,* 94)

I like the way The Merriam-Webster online dictionary defines rapture as "an expression or manifestation of ecstasy or passion ... a state or experience of being carried away by overwhelming emotion ... a mystical experience in which the spirit is exalted to a knowledge of divine things" (*Merriam-Webster.com.* 1 July 2014). And Rev. Moon uses the word rapture to describe our ultimate relationship with God, "Sharing joy with God is more rapturous and intoxicating than owning all of heaven and earth. (*Cheon Seong Gyeong* p 281) When the Lord returns, those who are aspiring towards oneness with God will be caught up with these emotions. Their spirits will be lifted up to meet Christ at his second coming.

6. The sun will be darkened, the moon will not give light, and the stars will fall from heaven.

Jesus said that in the Last Days, "Immediately after the tribulation of those days shall the sun be darkened, and the moon shall not give her light, and the stars shall fall from heaven, and the powers of the heavens shall be shaken" (Matthew 24:29).

Sometimes we hear scary news about an imminent cosmic cataclysm that could occur in our solar system, and we can conjecture that of course this could happen. However, is it possible for stars to fall from heaven into the earth? This is impossible, given the fact that the earth is far smaller than the stars. The Divine Principle says that this is also not meant to be taken literally.

It is written that Joseph, the eleventh of the twelve sons of Jacob, had a dream:

> And he dreamed yet another dream, and told it to his brethren, and said, Behold, I have dreamed a dream more; and, behold, the sun and the moon and the eleven stars made obeisance to me. And he told it to his father, and to his brethren: and his father rebuked him, and said unto him, What is this dream that thou hast dreamed? Shall I and thy mother and thy brethren indeed come to bow down ourselves to thee to the earth? (Genesis 37:9-10)

Joseph's dream became a reality when he became the prime minister of Egypt. His parents and brothers bowed down before him. In his dream, the sun and moon symbolized the parents, while the stars symbolized their children. The Divine Principle explains in detail that Jesus and the Holy Spirit function together as True Parents who came to give spiritual rebirth to humanity. Therefore, the sun and the moon represent Jesus and the Holy Spirit, while the stars represent the faithful believers who are their children. John 1:9 talks about the true Light. The light of the words of Jesus is the sunlight. The light of the Holy Spirit, who came as the Spirit of truth, is the moonlight.

The Divine Principle explains:

> For the sun to be darkened and the moon to lose its light means that the New Testament Word given by Jesus and the Holy Spirit will lose its luster. How can the Word as revealed in the New Testament possibly lose its light? The Old Testament Word was eclipsed when Jesus and the Holy Spirit came and gave us the New Testament Word, which fulfilled the Old Testament Word (2 Corinthians 3:7-11). Likewise, when Christ returns and gives the new truth in order to fulfill the New Testament Word and build a new heaven and new earth, the Word that he gave at his first coming will lose its light. It is said that the Word will lose its light because, with the coming of a new era, the period of the mission of the old truth will have lapsed.

The prophecy that the stars will fall from heaven signifies that in the Last Days many faithful Christian believers will make a misstep and fall from God's grace. At the time of Jesus, the chosen people were all yearning for the coming of the Messiah, but they met their downfall when they did not recognize Jesus as the Messiah and opposed him. Likewise, Christians who have been anxiously awaiting the return of Jesus are likely to make the same misjudgment and fail to recognize him when he actually returns.

Jesus asked, "Nevertheless, when the Son of man comes, will he find faith on earth?" (Luke 18:8) On another occasion, he said he would declare to devout believers, "I never knew you; depart from me, you evil-doers." (Matthew 7:23) Jesus gave these warnings to the Christians of the Last Days because he foresaw that they would be likely to disbelieve and trespass against him at his Second Advent. (*Exposition of the Divine Principle,* 95)

I know that there is a theory of the origin of the universe that predicts time itself will end in just five billion years—coincidentally, right around the time our sun is slated to die. I don't dismiss the possibility, but what the Divine Principle points out is that the destruction of the earth, which is mentioned in the Bible in the last days, signifies the end of the evil sovereignty and the start of a new sovereignty - or the end of an era and the beginning of a new one filled with hope. Contrary to this, many Christians believe that God will end the entire human race, along with the entire universe, then every person will face judgment to determine whether their spirits will eternally dwell in heaven or in hell.

If the earth will indeed come to a literal end, then it seems logical to surmise that there will always be a place – somewhere in the universe – where the human race will continue to exist as God created us to be His children and to be the substantial body through which he could enjoy his creation. To God, this relationship is eternal.

Is Jesus God or Man?

First, I would like to say that we, as Unificationists, revere Jesus with all our hearts as the first man to receive God's love as a son - or as 'God's only begotten Son'. If you recall earlier, I mentioned that it was Jesus who guided Sun Myung Moon to discover the Divine Principle. Understanding the heart of Jesus is a prerequisite to understanding the Divine Principle fully. If you attend a Divine Principle presentation on Jesus' life and mission, you'll most likely weep deeply when you understand his sorrowful heart. Many of our members had never accepted Jesus Christ as their Savior, but when they heard the Divine Principle, they welcomed Jesus into their lives with a new and fresh perspective.

Is Jesus God?

Christians are divided over this argument, although a majority believe that Jesus *is* quite literally God. Several verses in the Bible seemingly suggest that Jesus is God. In John 14:9 Jesus said, "He that hath seen me hath seen the Father." It appears that Jesus was saying that he is God. However, we can find verses in the Bible that explain that Jesus is not God Himself. For example:

> For there is one God, and one mediator between God and men, the man Christ Jesus. (1 Timothy 2:5)

It doesn't get any clearer than this. "For there is one God" means, of course, only one! Notice that it says, "...one mediator between God and mankind, the man Christ Jesus."

If Jesus is not God, what kind of being is he? Jesus is a human being without original sin. He came to restore what Adam failed to do. These verses support this:

> For as by one man's [Adam's] disobedience many were made sinners, so by the obedience of one [Jesus] shall many be made righteous. (Romans 5:19)

> For since by man [Adam] came death, by man [Jesus] came also the resurrection of the dead. (1 Corinthians 15:21)

Thus, Jesus is a man. But, he is not an ordinary man because he is a part of God's lineage. Jesus is a true man, the perfected Adam. He came as the Messiah. So, what kind of a man is the Messiah? The Messiah's mission is to restore what Adam failed to fulfill. Adam failed to reach perfection. Jesus came and perfected himself as the perfected Adam. Jesus resembles God himself, because he is perfect.

If we look at John 14:9 at a different angle, the verse also suggests that Jesus Christ is not God himself. However, he is the manifestation and the image of God—"he that hath seen me hath seen the Father." The following verse tells us that God dwells in Jesus Christ:

> Believest thou not that I am in the Father, and the Father in me? the words that I speak unto you I speak not of myself: but the Father that dwelleth in me, he doeth the works. (John 14:10)

What is the difference between Jesus and us? We are the result of the Fall. We inherited the blood lineage from a false father - Satan. We have original sin. Jesus was born without original sin. This is why he is referred to as the only begotten son: "For God so loved the world that he gave his only begotten Son, that whosoever believeth in him should not perish, but have everlasting life" (John 3:16).

So, is there a problem calling Jesus God? I don't think so, because God manifests through Jesus. The only problem I have with this is that our relationship with Jesus can become impersonal and distant as we put him high up on the pedestal of the cross. Thankfully, I now have a more personal relationship with Jesus. Jesus now feels to me like a real friend and an elder brother, and not just as an unreachable supernatural being, although he had the ability to perform miracles due to his oneness with God. Jesus was a human being, just like us, a person who had flesh, who thirsted, got hungry, joked, laughed, raised his voice, needed to go to sleep, and most of all someone who desired love just like anyone else. We are all meant to have the relationship to God that he enjoyed. He came as the prototype, the model for us to follow - not just worship.

It is God's desire to dwell on earth through His sons and daughters. God is invisible. He made Himself visible and manifests through His son Jesus. We, too, can become God's manifestation, but only if we are perfect in character as our heavenly Father is perfect. Therefore, Jesus said, "Be ye therefore perfect, even as your Father which is in heaven is perfect" (Matthew 5:48). In other words, we have to reach the level of spiritual maturity where our character resonates with God's. Let me make it clear, however, that 'perfect' does not refer to a state of being in which we do not make ordinary human mistakes, rather it refers to a state in which we reach our full human God-given potential.

Jesus Did Not Come to Die on the Cross

"Crucifixion is a form of slow and painful execution in which the victim is tied or nailed to a large wooden cross and left to hang until dead. It is principally known from antiquity, but remains in occasional use in some countries." (Wikipedia.com, 5 July 2014)

Here are the conventional beliefs about Jesus' crucifixion:

1. Jesus came to die on the cross.
2. Jesus' crucifixion brought complete salvation to man and nothing further was needed.

The majority, if not all, Christians believe that Jesus Christ came to earth to die on the cross, and that this was the will of God and that his crucifixion was the ultimate salvation. The Divine Principle says otherwise:

1. Jesus did *not* come to die on the cross.

What you read below are my notes taken from Divine Principle lecturers explaining about the travesty of Jesus' crucifixion:

One thing is clear to all Christian believers: Jesus is the Messiah, born with the mission to bring salvation to a suffering world. But what does it mean to bring salvation? What does it mean to save someone? If a man fell out of a boat and was drowning, to save him you would help him back into the boat. If someone ate poison, salvation would be to take the poison out of his or her system. In other words, salvation means to restore a person to where they were before they fell into danger.

Let's begin with the question, "What exactly is it that humanity needs to be saved from?" The answer, if we understand the Fall and how we became separated from God, is clear. We need to be saved from being a member of this dysfunctional human family. We need to be saved from a family that, instead of being rooted in God's love, is rooted in a fallen, selfish love initiated by the fallen archangel. This is a family that passes on to its children an imperfect and distorted love and fallen nature.

What then does this tell us about salvation? If we want to leave the sinful family we are a part of, then naturally we would first seek an alternative—a godly family that we could join.

There needs to be a family that belongs to God and is rooted in God's love, a family through which we can restore our original God-given nature. In other words, salvation means to join a family where we can fulfill God's original purpose of creation. This is where we can grow to become God's true children, where we can become parents able to give birth to children free of sin, and where our children can grow up to be lords of creation establishing and sustaining a world of peace.

God needs a man and a woman who can overcome temptation and stand as God's true son and daughter. Jesus came to be that True Son. And not only was he God's son, according to his words in Matthew 9:15, he was the bridegroom who had come to find his bride. Had the people welcomed Jesus, he would have been able to meet his bride, the woman who was to become God's true daughter. Together, they would have formed God's true family. And through this family God would have been able to save

43

all humanity. Jesus and his bride would have stood as the True Parents of humankind. They would have been able to invite all people to leave the fallen archangel who had taken the position of the false parent and be adopted into God's family. In Romans 8:23, St. Paul described this final step of redemption and adoption. Beginning with the people of Israel, Jesus and his bride would have brought all the people of the world into God's family.

In fact, Jesus first desire was **not** to be crucified. Our lecturers further explained:

What did Jesus teach that we must do in order to gain salvation? The first and most essential point that Jesus made concerning our salvation is that we believe in him. In the fullest sense, we are asked to unite with Jesus—in our beliefs, our actions, and in our hearts. In John 6:28, when asked by the people what they must do to do the work of God, Jesus told them to believe in him, the one whom God has sent. In Luke 18:18, when asked by one man, how he could gain eternal life, Jesus told him to give all he had to the poor and then follow him. And in Matthew 11:37 Jesus taught that if we want to become his disciples, we must love him even more than we love our own life.

Jesus never taught that rejecting and killing him was a good thing. In fact, when people did reject Jesus, he strongly condemned them. He made it clear that because they had rejected him, they would not find their way to Heaven.

Reverend Sun Myung Moon said: "Jesus Christ did not come to repeat the Mosaic Law. He came to pronounce a new law of God. People missed the whole point. And Jesus was accused." And sadly, that is what happened. The chosen people rejected Jesus. Take for example, Judas, Jesus' betrayer. Jesus told him it would have been better if he had never been born. Or consider Matthew 11:20-24, when people in the towns where his great works were performed refused to repent. This was very painful for Jesus. It meant that God's will to bring peace to this world would not be accomplished. It meant that there would be more tragedy and more suffering. For this reason, Jesus proclaimed that they would find themselves deeper in Hell than the people of Sodom and Gomorrah.

And there are other examples. In Luke 19:41-44, Jesus, in tears, spoke of the terrible suffering the chosen people would experience because they had not recognized his coming. The desire of Jesus' heart was that the people receive him.

On the cross, Jesus did not proclaim that the people were fulfilling God's will. He made it clear that they were doing something terribly wrong. This is why he asked God to forgive them.

When Jesus first started his ministry, in Matthew 4:17 and 4:23, he proclaimed that the Kingdom of God was at hand. This was the message of the victorious Messiah who is received by the people. After he had received John's baptism, when he gave his first reading from scripture in the synagogue at Nazareth, he quoted from Isaiah 61, which prophesied the glorious coming of the Messiah as "king of kings, and lord of lords."

The crucifixion was not the result of God's first plan. It was instead the result of His son being rejected by the chosen people, just as Moses was rejected.

The question that often comes when we say this is—"If God wanted Jesus to be received and accepted, then why did God let that happen?"

45

We know God prepared the foundation for Jesus' ministry. However, as we have learned God has given us a portion of responsibility, especially when it comes to love. Just as God could not force Adam and Eve to love Him, God could not force the people to love, believe in, and follow Jesus. The biblical history from Adam to Abraham and then from Abraham to the birth of Jesus is a story of God preparing a people to receive the Messiah.

Think about it. Was God's primary objective in history to prepare people to kill His son? No. If the key to salvation was the death of God's son—that could have happened from the beginning, when Cain murdered Abel.

God knows that it is the nature of evil to destroy the good. That is why it took so long for God to send Jesus. God did not want to send His son until He had prepared a situation in which Jesus could avoid being killed. God's goal was to prepare an environment that would protect Jesus from the evils of this world.

There can be no doubt that God was working to raise up a people of faith, a people able to receive the Messiah. If you asked the people of faith at the time of Jesus, "Does God want you to receive the Messiah or kill him?" they would all say that God wants us to receive him. Only people on the side of evil, such as King Herod, wanted to kill the Messiah.

Jesus was killed not because he was the Messiah. He was killed because the people did not realize who he was. They thought he was a false prophet, a blasphemer, a threat to their established religion and practices.

If God had originally predestined His son to die on the cross, Jesus would have expected to go that path as his ultimate course and welcomed it! Why, then, did he desperately pray three times in the Garden of Gethsemane prior to his crucifixion these words?

> And he went a little farther, and fell on his face, and prayed, saying, O my Father, if it be possible, let this cup pass from me: nevertheless not as I will, but as thou wilt. (Matthew 26:39)

Jesus did not utter those desperate words out of his fear of being crucified. In truth, Jesus offered those desperate prayers because he knew well that his death would shatter the hope of attaining the Kingdom of Heaven on earth with his generation. This would be a tragic disappointment to God, who had worked laboriously to realize this hope through the long ages since the Fall. Furthermore, Jesus knew that humanity's afflictions would continue unrelieved until the time of his Second Coming.

2. Jesus' crucifixion did *not* bring complete salvation.

Was Jesus' sacrifice on the cross for naught? Of course not. If it were, Christianity would not have brought forth its illustrious history. However, salvation was not completed on the cross. If it was why would the world be in such a state?

Here are more notes from the Divine Principle lecturer:

> *Jesus was crucified. But what is so incredible is that while being put to death on the cross, Jesus continued to love those who persecuted him, asking God to forgive them. No one in human history has been ever able to love his or her enemy as Jesus did. Jesus transformed his death into a life-giving offering. Although his body was killed, his spirit was taken by God. Jesus' love created a realm of*

resurrection that all humankind can enter through faith in him.

Because of Jesus' victory, those who believe in him and follow his teachings receive the Holy Spirit and experience God's love and forgiveness. We call this "spiritual salvation." By going to the cross, Jesus could not bring God's Kingdom substantially on the earth, but he was able to bring believers spiritually to God.

Sadly, spiritual salvation has its limits. On this earth, Christians must be saved like any other child born into this fallen world. This is why St. Paul lamented his own struggle with sin. In Romans 7:24-25 he cried out, "Wretched man that I am, who will deliver me from this body of death? ... with my mind I myself serve the law of God; but with the flesh the law of sin." And this is why he acknowledged in Romans 8:23 that our salvation in the physical body would not come until sometime in the future when our adoption by God would be complete.

With the root remaining corrupt, the whole tree of humankind continues to suffer the effects of sin—war, hunger, poverty, and so forth.

This is the limit of salvation through the cross. And because it is limited, we can now understand more clearly why the Messiah needs to come a second time on this earth. God must send a Messiah again in order to fulfill His original plan, His Ideal of Creation. This is why Jesus taught us in Matthew 6:10 to pray, "Thy will be done on earth as it is in heaven."

John the Baptist's Role in the Crucifixion of Jesus

According to conventional Christian beliefs, John the Baptist was a great prophet who fulfilled his mission to serve the Messiah. However, the Divine Principle explains that John the Baptist played a major role in Jesus' being misunderstood by the Jewish people and his resulting crucifixion. Here are more quotes from my notes from our Divine Principle lecturers:

How did God expect the people to know that Jesus was the Messiah? That was the mission that God gave John the Baptist. John the Baptist's mission was to prepare the way for Jesus. John the Baptist is the one who was to announce to the world that Jesus was the Messiah.

If we look at the history leading up to Jesus' birth, we can clearly recognize God's effort to prepare a people able to receive His son. The preparation really began in Abraham's family, two thousand years before the birth of Christ. Abraham and his son Isaac showed great faith in God. And then Isaac's sons, Esau and Jacob were able to overcome their fallen nature and embrace after twenty-one years of animosity. For this reason, God renamed Jacob Israel. And God determined that he would send the Messiah to the descendants of Abraham, Isaac, and Jacob. But, in a world where there were kingdoms and empires with great armies, a foundation of one family was not enough. God needed to raise up a people and a kingdom that would be able to receive His son. So, after the Israelites had spent four hundred years in Egypt, God sent Moses to bring them out of Egypt to the land of Canaan to form a nation. In Canaan, centered on Moses and the laws God had given him (I am referring to the Ten Commandments), God was planning to send the Messiah. But the people rebelled against Moses and he eventually died in the wilderness.

Four hundred years later, God tried again to prepare a foundation for the Messiah through the kings Saul, David, and Solomon. God's hope was that the Kings would unite the people around the Temple. For that purpose, God had the kings build the Temple. The Temple was a symbol of the coming Messiah. In it the word of God and the Ten Commandments were kept. This would prepare the people to unite with the Messiah when he came. But, the Kings failed to do God's will. The third king, Solomon, built the Temple, but corrupted it with evil forms of worship. Later this would lead to extremes such as the sacrifice of children as offerings to false gods.

To remedy this, God sent prophets. One famous one that you may have heard of was Elijah. God wanted the prophets to turn the people back to God's word and the Temple. But Israel rejected the prophets and was eventually invaded by outside forces. The Temple was destroyed, and the people were taken into captivity in Babylon.

In Babylon, the Israelites repented of their sins and eventually were able to return to Jerusalem to rebuild their city and the second Temple. Nehemiah and Malachi revived God's words.

Through the prophet Malachi, in the last book of the Hebrew Scriptures, God proclaims that the Messiah will come, but first, God will send the prophet Elijah once again to turn the hearts of the fathers to their children and hearts of the children to their fathers and prepare a people for the Lord.

And God gave a warning—if this does not happen, a curse will come on the land. Four hundred years later, Jesus was born. But what about the return of Elijah who had to come first to prepare the people's hearts?

Now, let's talk about John the Baptist. His story is in the Gospel of Luke. Four hundred years after Malachi, an angel appeared in the Temple and spoke to Zechariah the *chief priest on duty that year. The angel told him that his wife, Elizabeth, who had been unable to have children, that she would give birth to a son he should name John and that this child would go forth with the spirit and power of Elijah. This means that John was actually the "Elijah" that God had promised He would send before the coming of the Messiah.*

John grew up and eventually went into the wilderness to fast and pray. There, God told him that He would show him the Messiah. With that news, John came out of the wilderness to the river Jordan, and there, with great excitement, began to proclaim the news that "the Kingdom of God is at hand." Jesus, at the age of 30, came to be baptized. When Jesus emerged from the water, John saw God's spirit came upon Jesus and he heard the voice of God say, "This is my son in whom I am well pleased," and John testified that Jesus was the Messiah.

At this point, what was God expecting to happen? God intended for John to humble himself and believe in, follow, and love Jesus. He was to have been Jesus' first disciple. And then John's associates, people of faith, people who had been longing and waiting for the Messiah, would have all become disciples of Jesus. But that never happened. In fact, one of the reasons Jesus was rejected was that Jesus testified to himself. (John 8:13) According to Jewish law at that time, there had to be at least two witnesses to prove something. John and his disciples should have been those witnesses.

We know that when Jesus went to the synagogue in Nazareth and testified to himself, the people wanted to stone him. If I were to boast to you that I am the world's greatest teacher, you would be critical before I said another word. But if someone you respected deeply told you that I am a great teacher, then you would at least want to listen and hear me out.

John, not Jesus, should have gone to the synagogue to proclaim that Jesus was the Messiah. They all knew John was a prophet of God. They knew about his birth, that it was announced by an angel of God. If John had told the people that Jesus was the Messiah, Israel could have received Jesus, and not only Israel. Through Israel, Jesus could have reached out to the East, where the wise men who had brought gifts at his birth had come from. God had prepared those lands as well. And eventually, even Rome could have been transformed through this new teaching. Judaism was widespread and very influential throughout the empire. This is how Jesus could have become the victorious living Messiah. As the Messiah, he would have taken a bride and established God's family rooted in God's love. In this way, Jesus and his bride, standing as the True Parents of humanity, would have begun God's kingdom here on earth.

But what happened? John did not follow Jesus. After he testified to Jesus, he went his own way. He kept his own disciples. In Matthew 9:14, we read how John's disciples criticized Jesus, and his disciples, because they were not fasting.

And John's teachings differed from the Gospel. John was teaching the laws of Moses according to the old way. Jesus was teaching a new way. When Mary Magdalene was caught in the act of adultery, according to the law, she was supposed to be stoned to death. But Jesus said, "He that is without sin among you, let him first cast a stone at her" (John 8:7). If you check the New Testament accounts, you will find that at that time John was casting stones at *the king's house, accusing the king of adultery. So the king threw him into prison.*

When John was in prison, he sent his disciples to Jesus to ask if he were the Messiah or not, revealing that he had lost faith in Jesus or at least had serious doubts about who he was.. Matthew 11:3 says, "And said unto him, Art thou he that should come, or do we look for another?" This was the same John who was told directly by God who Jesus was, and who had earlier testified that Jesus was the Messiah. Jesus was not very happy with John's interrogation. He then replied, "Go back and report to John what you hear and see: The blind receive sight, the lame walk, those who have leprosy are cleansed, the deaf hear, the dead are raised, and the good news is proclaimed to the poor. Blessed is anyone who does not stumble on account of me." These verses make it appear as if Jesus was very disappointed in John's doubt. The following verse shows that because of John the Baptist's failure to unite with Jesus, he was judged harshly by him:

> Verily I say unto you, among them that are born of women there hath not risen a greater than John the Baptist: notwithstanding he that is least in the kingdom of heaven is greater than he. (Matthew 11:11)

John the Baptist was deemed the greatest, but because of his failure, his status was reduced to the lowest state. And in the following verse, Jesus reiterates that the world suffered because of his loss of faith:

> And from the days of John the Baptist until now the kingdom of heaven suffereth violence, and the violent take it by force. (Matthew 11:12)

The Divine Principle lecturer said:

In addition to not following Jesus, John outright denied being Elijah. This is recorded in John 1:21: "They asked him, 'Then who are you? Are you Elijah?' He said, 'I am not.' 'Are you the Prophet?' He answered, 'No.'" This was a serious problem for Jesus, because later, when Jesus was asked, "If you are the Messiah, then where is Elijah, who, according to scripture, must come first?" Jesus answered that John the Baptist was Elijah:

> *"And his disciples asked him, saying, Why then say the scribes that Elias must first come? And Jesus answered and said unto them, Elias truly shall first come, and restore all things. But I say unto you, That Elias is come already, and they knew him not, but have done unto him whatsoever they listed. Likewise shall also the Son of man suffer of them. Then the disciples understood that he spake unto them of John the Baptist." (Matthew 17:10-13)*

According to Luke 3:4-6, John was the voice in the wilderness preparing the way for the Lord, to make the way straight and smooth, to make that runway upon which Jesus could land. But instead, John the Baptist blocked the way to Jesus. When John, the highly respected and educated son of a priest, denied that he was Elijah, he made Jesus, the uneducated son of a carpenter, appear to be a false Messiah. John's words and actions made it impossible for those who believed in scripture to believe in Jesus.

After John was killed in prison, what could Jesus do? He had to find someone else to testify to him. But because of John's failure, none of the religious leaders God had loved and prepared was willing to stand up for Jesus. And so Jesus gathered disciples from the common people, people who may have been uneducated, but who had sincere hearts. At one point he took the three disciples who were closest to him, Peter, James and John, up on a mountain, called the Mount of Transfiguration. On this mountain they saw Moses and Elijah from the spirit world and heard God's voice saying, "This is my beloved Son, in whom I am well pleased; hear ye him" (Matthew 17:5). These were the words God had spoken to John the Baptist, but because he failed to testify for Jesus, the same words were instructed to Jesus' new disciples in place of John the Baptist.

If these disciples had been faithful to Jesus, believed in, and followed him, there would have been a way for Jesus to continue on the path as the living Messiah. But, tragically, even they were not able to sustain their faith. Just before he was arrested, Jesus took these same disciples late at night to the Garden of Gethsemane. There, he gave them an opportunity to show their faith and love for him. He asked them to stay awake and watch while he prayed for God to open another way to go other than the way of the cross. He prayed because he knew that if he went the path of the cross, evil would continue to dominate this world. Evil would attack his followers in the future with persecution and death. He also foresaw that the chosen people of Israel would suffer greatly. He knew that all humanity would have to go through a tragic course, and God's heart would be broken again. But, God did not answer his prayer. Why? It's because the disciples slept. They were not able to demonstrate their love for Jesus. Jesus woke them up, chastised them, and asked them to stay awake just this hour. He prayed again the same prayer, *but again the disciples slept. He tried a third time, but the disciples slept again. It was clear no one on this earth truly loved Jesus more than his or her own life. Furthermore, Jesus' main disciple, Peter, would later deny that he knew Jesus three times.*

This is why Jesus had to go the way of the cross. The faithlessness at Moses' time was repeated in Jesus' time. And so, as Moses lifted up the serpent, Jesus had to be lifted up on the cross, and on the cross Jesus won a victory of love. He loved humankind. He loved those who deserved to perish. He loved us and asked God to forgive us. This is what enabled God to resurrect Jesus.

While Jesus hung on the cross, no one understood the full extent of his suffering except God alone. However, the cross was a very painful sight for God who could not bear to look at His son dying; God even turned His back on His son who cried out:

> And about the ninth hour Jesus cried with a loud voice, saying, Eli, Eli, lama sabachthani? that is to say, My God, my God, why hast thou forsaken me?
> (Matthew 27:46)

During his lifetime, Reverend Sun Myung Moon encouraged all Christian ministers to look at the significance of Jesus' crucifixion with a new and deeper perspective. As a result, some of those churches took down their crosses and replaced them with crowns to represent Jesus' victory through his resurrection.

I was asked if Unificationists believe that the cross is evil. My answer is, "Absolutely not." Jesus offered his life and gave forgiveness through the cross. Although the crucifixion represented a spiritual victory against Satan on the one hand, it was a very painful tragedy on the other. For this reason, Unificationists focus more on the celebration of Jesus' resurrection rather than on the celebration of Jesus' crucifixion.

When God works with people, He always has a Plan A and a Plan B, if you will. As I explained earlier, God gave us a portion of responsibility to carry out His providence which is to return to His ideal. Whenever God makes plans that involve people, we have to do our part, but there is always the possibility that we won't. This explains why there are two types of prophecies concerning the coming of the Messiah. One type, found in the book of Isaiah, predicts a glorious Messiah who will establish God's Kingdom on the earth in reality:

> For unto us a child is born, unto us a son is given: and the government shall be upon his shoulder: and his name shall be called Wonderful, Counsellor, The mighty God, The everlasting Father, The Prince of Peace. Of the increase of his government and peace there shall be no end, upon the throne of David, and upon his kingdom, to order it, and to establish it with judgment and with justice from henceforth even forever. The zeal of the Lord of hosts will perform this. (Isaiah 9:6-7)

> And in that day there shall be a root of Jesse, which shall stand for an ensign of the people; to it shall the Gentiles seek: and his rest shall be glorious. And it shall come to pass in that day, that the Lord shall set his hand again the second time to recover the remnant of his people, which shall be left, from Assyria, and from Egypt, and from Pathros, and from Cush, and from Elam, and from Shinar, and from Hamath, and

from the islands of the sea. And he shall set up an ensign for the nations, and shall assemble the outcasts of Israel, and gather together the dispersed of Judah from the four corners of the earth. (Isaiah 11:10-12)

This is what *would* have happened if the people had believed in Jesus and fulfilled their part.

Conversely, the *other* prophecy found in Isaiah reveals God's secondary plan—what will happen if people fail to do their part? This quote predicts a Messiah who will suffer in order to pay the price for humanity's errant ways:

He is despised and rejected of men; a man of sorrows, and acquainted with grief: and we hid as it were our faces from him; he was despised, and we esteemed him not. (Isaiah 53:3)

Sadly, the people at Jesus' time rejected the Messiah. In the Garden of Gethsemane, Jesus made his very last appeal. He prayed deeply to God not to be crucified. He knew that God's heart would be broken if he took the cup of death. He knew that the chosen people and his followers would suffer tremendous persecution. Unfortunately, no one stood up for him, not even his own disciples. Jesus had no other choice to save humanity but to go the way of the cross. This explains why when Simon Peter drew a sword and struck the high priest's servant, Jesus chastised him, "Put up thy sword into the sheath: the cup which my Father hath given me, shall I not drink it?" (John 18:11). By that time, Jesus had already made the heart wrenching decision to go the way of the cross.

Reverend Sun Myung Moon said:

People say that Jesus came to die. Was his death indeed predestined by God, or was it an event brought on by circumstances? You should know that it was something that happened suddenly and unexpectedly. We can discern this from the New Testament's account of the Transfiguration: "And behold, two men talked with him, Moses and Elijah, who appeared in glory and spoke of his departure [his crucifixion] which he was to accomplish in Jerusalem" (Luke 9:30-31).

When Jesus later informed Peter that he would suffer in Jerusalem and be crucified, Peter violently protested, "God forbid, Lord! This shall never happen to you!" (Matthew 16:22). Then Jesus lashed out at him, saying, "Get behind me, Satan! You are a hindrance to me; for you are not on the side of God but of men" (Matthew 16:23).

Conventional Christians understand this passage to mean that Jesus was supposed to die on the cross, and because Peter tried to stop him, Jesus called him "Satan." What Jesus actually meant was this: Peter had witnessed the trance-like scene on the Mount of Transfiguration alongside Jesus; hence, he should have heard some time during that event, the instruction to Jesus that he should go to his death. However, Peter had dozed off and never heard it. Yet now that Jesus' death was decided, Peter had no grounds telling Jesus what to do or not to do.

The decision [to alter Jesus' course] had been made on the Mount of Transfiguration. Jesus had originally come to fulfill God's Will both spiritually and physically, but he was driven into a situation where unless he sacrificed himself, he would have to turn the nation and the people over to Satan. In that situation, by going the way of crucifixion God strove to lay at least a spiritual foundation. In other words, God had determined to lead him on a secondary dispensation, one that would give birth to Christianity. (73:218, September 18, 1974; World Scriptures and the Teachings of Sun Myung Moon, 507-508; Universal Peace Federation; Copyright 2007)

Predestination

Predestination, in theology, is the doctrine that asserts that all events have been willed by God. John Calvin interpreted biblical predestination to mean that God willed eternal damnation for some people and salvation for others. (Wikipedia.org, 6 July 2014)

The belief that everything that will happen has already been decided by God or fate and cannot be changed. (*Merriam-Webster.com*. 6 July 2014)

Theological controversies over predestination have caused great confusion in the religious lives of many people. In Christianity, particularly because of John Calvin, some believe that God long ago determined who would be saved and who would be damned regardless of their merit or lack thereof.

We can find many passages in the Bible that are often interpreted to mean that everything in an individual's life, such as prosperity and decline, happiness and misery, salvation and damnation, as well as the rise and fall of nations comes to pass exactly as predestined by God. St. Paul wrote to the Romans:

For he saith to Moses, I will have mercy on whom I will have mercy, and I will have compassion on whom I will have compassion. So then it is not of him that willeth, nor of him that runneth, but of God that sheweth mercy. (Romans 9:15-16)

> Hath not the potter power over the clay, of the same lump to make one vessel unto honour, and another unto dishonour? (Romans 9:21)

These verses make it appear as if God is an unfair God. This would mean that no matter how we strive not to be damned, it wouldn't matter because it is all about God's will. If we believe in the doctrine of absolute predestination, it is easy to blame God for any misfortune that happens in our lives.

The Divine Principle explains that not everything is a result of God's absolute predestination. How does it clarify this issue? Simply said, since God is a good God, He predestines everything for goodness only. However, God's predestination cannot be completed without us taking our part in fulfilling our responsibilities. God has given us responsibilities and the freedom to choose. The Divine Principle says:

> Yet we can also find sufficient evidence in the Bible to refute the doctrine of absolute predestination. For example, God warned the first human ancestors not to eat of the fruit in order to prevent their Fall (Genesis 2:17). We can deduce from this that the human Fall was not the outcome of God's predestination, but rather the result of man's disobedience to God's commandment. Again we read, "the Lord was sorry that he had made man on the earth and it grieved him to his heart" (Genesis 6:6). If God predestined the human Fall, there would be no reason for Him to grieve over fallen human beings, who were acting in accordance with His predestination.
>
> The doctrine that the outcome of human undertakings is determined not by God's predestation, but instead by human effort, is supported by the well-known biblical verse, "Ask, and it will be given you; seek, and you will find; knock, and it will be opened to you"

(Matthew 7:7). If every human undertaking were to turn out as God had predestined, why did Jesus emphasize the need for human effort? The Bible instructs us to pray for our sick brothers (James 5:14-15), suggesting that illness and health do not depend solely on God's predestination. If everything were determined by inevitable fate, as predestined by God, our tearful supplications would be to no avail.

We would expect that since God is absolute, when He has predestined something, it is fixed absolutely and cannot be altered by human effort. Therefore, if we accept the traditional doctrine that all things are absolutely predestined by God, then we have to conclude that no human endeavor, including prayer, evangelism, or charity, can add anything more to God's providence of restoration. Any extra effort beyond the natural course of events would be completely useless. (*Exposition of the Divine Principle,* 154)

This diagram below explains that God predestines everything and every one of us to fulfill our purpose of life. However, His predestination cannot be fulfilled without us fulfilling our responsibility.

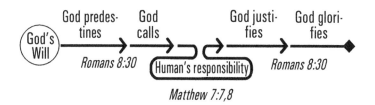

Matthew 7:7,8

Romans 8:30 - "Moreover whom he did predestinate, them he also called: and whom he called, them he also justified: and whom he justified, them he also glorified."

63

Matthew 7:7,8 - Ask, and it shall be given you; seek, and ye shall find; knock, and it shall be opened unto you: For every one that asketh receiveth; and he that seeketh findeth; and to him that knocketh it shall be opened.

Faith Alone Won't Save Us

Some Christians believe that to receive salvation all we need is faith, that we are 'justified by faith alone'. We can read several passages in the Bible that support this understanding. Here are a few:

> Therefore we conclude that a man is justified by faith without the deeds of the law. (Romans 3:28)

> But to him that worketh not, but believeth on him that justifieth the ungodly, his faith is counted for righteousness. (Romans 4:5)

> And if by grace, then is it no more of works: otherwise grace is no more grace. But if it be of works, then it is no more grace: otherwise work is no more work. (Romans 11:6)

> For by grace are ye saved through faith; and that not of yourselves: it is the gift of God: Not of works, lest any man should boast. (Ephesians 2:8-9)

The *Exposition of the Divine Principle* does clearly explain that faith alone is not enough in light of understanding our portion of responsibility. To be saved, we need to have faith in God, and we need to do good for others. Thus, when asked which was the greatest commandment in the law, Jesus replied, "'Thou shalt love the Lord thy God with all thy heart, and with all thy soul, and with all thy mind. This is the first and great commandment. And the second is like unto it, Thou shalt love thy neighbour as thyself'" (Matthew 22:37-39).

The *Exposition of the Divine Principle* contains two sub-sections about faith and deeds. They are called the "Foundation of Faith" and "Foundation of Substance." They explain how God guided His central figures, such as the prophets and chosen leaders, throughout human history to lay the providential foundation in order to send the Messiah. These chapters also clearly explain why the providential events in the Bible were repeated under very similar conditions, albeit in different time periods. Historical events were repeated when God's chosen people, in the past, failed to lay the necessary foundations. God, therefore, had His central figures carry out similar tasks that the past central figures failed to accomplish, in order to establish every necessary foundation to receive the Messiah. An example of this is that when Ishmael and Isaac failed to unite to lay the Foundation of Faith and the Foundation of Substance, Jacob and Esau had to undergo a similar fate.

"Foundation of Faith" and "Foundation of Substance" have profound meaning, but in this book, I simply refer to these foundations as faith and good deeds. Both of these foundations are necessary to receive salvation.

When I give Divine Principle lectures, I always used the example of an airplane descending to the ground. In order for an airplane to land safely, it needs a good runway. Likewise, in order for the Messiah to come, he needs people to lay the necessary foundation for him to be able to accomplish God's will.

Faith alone is not enough. As the old saying goes, "if you're going to talk the talk, you've got to walk the walk," which means, "practice what you preach.' After all, the Bible says that we need more than faith alone. It also says that our good actions - *our good choices* - are essential, too:

Ye see then how that by works a man is justified, and not by faith only. (James 2:24)

For as the body without the spirit is dead, so faith without works is dead also. (James 2:26)

I could be a very religious person and full of faith, but if I don't do good things for people according to what Christ instructed I am not fulfilling my responsible part as God's co-creator and child. Without fulfilling our responsible part how can we really call ourselves children of God?

Will Christ Come Again - If So, How?

Many Christians these days are waiting for Christ's return from the clouds. They believe that Christ will descend with power and great glory, with angels blowing loud trumpets.

There are three very popular views of the Second Advent of Christ. One view is that on his return all of the saved, dead, or alive, will be literally lifted up to meet Jesus Christ in the air. This is commonly called the "Rapture":

> For the Lord himself shall descend from heaven with a shout, with the voice of the archangel, and with the trump of God: and the dead in Christ shall rise first: Then we which are alive and remain shall be caught up together with them in the clouds, to meet the Lord in the air: and so shall we ever be with the Lord. (1 Thessalonians 4:16-17)

> And then shall appear the sign of the Son of man in heaven: and then shall all the tribes of the earth mourn, and they shall see the Son of man coming in the clouds of heaven with power and great glory. And he shall send his angels with a great sound of a trumpet, and they shall gather together his elect from the four winds, from one end of heaven to the other. (Matthew 24:30-31)

Another view of Christ's return is he will come with the armies from heaven to smite the world with his flaming sword. Some call this event the "Armageddon":

And the armies which were in heaven followed him upon white horses, clothed in fine linen, white and clean. And out of his mouth goeth a sharp sword, that with it he should smite the nations: and he shall rule them with a rod of iron: and he treadeth the winepress of the fierceness and wrath of Almighty God. And he hath on his vesture and on his thigh a name written, King of Kings, and Lord of Lords. (Revelation 19:14-16)

And, the third is the total destruction of the earth:

Looking for and hasting unto the coming of the day of God, wherein the heavens being on fire shall be dissolved, and the elements shall melt with fervent heat? (2 Peter 3:12)

Immediately after the tribulation of those days shall the sun be darkened, and the moon shall not give her light, and the stars shall fall from heaven, and the powers of the heavens shall be shaken. (Matthew 24:29)

If we adhere to these prophecies as literal, these events may seem to contradict each other. Why? Rapture is seemingly a peaceful occurrence, but Armageddon and total destruction are both violent events to be feared.

The Divine Principle has a different interpretation of the manner in which Christ will return. We read in the Old Testament that before Jesus appeared the prophet Malachi prophesied that Elijah would return before the coming of the Messiah: "Behold, I will send you Elijah the prophet before the coming of the great and dreadful day of the Lord" (Malachi 4:5).

Who was Elijah? Elijah was a great prophet in the northern kingdom of Israel in the 9th century B.C. He defended the worship of God over that of the Canaanite god Baal. He brought fire down from the sky, and was taken up in a chariot and horses of flames into heaven (2 Kings 2:11).

As the people eagerly awaited the coming of the Messiah, they also eagerly awaited for the coming of Elijah, who was to come first. Many believed that Elijah, who had ascended to heaven, would come down from heaven in the same way he had ascended. But contrary to their expectation, Jesus boldly claimed that John the Baptist was the Elijah whom they were waiting for. "And if you are willing to accept it, he is the Elijah who was to come." (Matthew 11:14).

The return of Elijah was never meant to take place in the miraculous manner that the chosen people expected. First of all, if we look at other Bible translation of 2 Kings 2:11, Elijah was said to be lifted up to heaven by a "chariot of fire," which - again is not a literal unscientific event but a symbolic one. The Divine Principle interpretation is that Elijah's body would be turned to ashes, but his spirit would be lifted up to heaven. Elijah's return - in other words - John the Baptist who came with his mission - occurred as a normal human birth. Resultantly, from this fact of John the Baptist's birth as a man, we can learn how Christ will come again as well.

Christ Will Return - Born as a Child

Revelation 12:5 reads: "And she brought forth a man child, who was to rule all nations with a rod of iron: and her child was caught up unto God, and to his throne." The child signifies the Lord of the Second Advent who rules all nations. The rod of iron here signifies the Word of God, with which the Lord will judge the sinful world and restore the

Kingdom of Heaven on earth. Hence, the Word of Christ will be our judge on the Last Day. "The word that I have spoken, the same shall judge him in the last day." (John 12:48).

Just as during the time of Jesus when Jewish people looked heavenward for Elijah, many Christians these days are gazing up to the clouds expecting the Lord's return. However, what we have learned about the actual return of Elijah tells us that Christ's return will be fulfilled when he is born as a child in the same manner of the First Coming.

This is what the Divine Principle says about Christ's return:

> At the First Coming of Jesus, many of the learned men of Israel thought that the Messiah would be born in Bethlehem as a descendant of King David (Matthew 2:5-6; Micah 5:2). Yet there were undoubtedly many other Jews who expected the Messiah to come on the clouds. This belief was based on their reading of the prophecy of Daniel, "I saw in the night visions, and behold, with the clouds of heaven there came one like a son of man" (Daniel 7:13) and other prophecies of supernatural events in the Last Days (i.e., Joel 2:30-31). Therefore, the Pharisees and Sadducees questioned Jesus, demanding that he show them a sign from heaven as proof that he was the Messiah (Matthew 16:1-4; Mark 8:11-12). Without any of the supernatural signs from heaven foretold in the Bible, they could not readily accept him as the long-awaited Messiah.
>
> Contrary to the expectations of many faithful Jews who believed on biblical grounds that the Messiah would come on the clouds with signs and portents in the heavens, Jesus was born on the earth as a child in a lowly family. Hence, we should re-examine the Bible from the perspective that the Second Advent of Christ may not take place in a miraculous way. It may, in fact, take place in the same manner as the First Advent. (*Exposition of the Divine Principle,* 384-385)

Jesus foretold what would happen to the Lord at his return. He gave us hints that the Lord of the Second Advent would not return in a supernatural way, but through the birth of a child. In other words, he would be human as Adam and Eve were and as you and I are.

Jesus foretold that when Christ returns, he will suffer first and be rejected: "But first he must suffer many things and be rejected by this generation" (Luke 17:25). If Jesus were to return literally on the clouds in a supernatural way with power and great glory and with the trumpets of angels according to what he said in Matthew 24:30-31, would he not readily be accepted and honored, even by this sin-ridden world? If he returned in such a manner, there is no way he would ever suffer persecution or rejection. Why, then, did Jesus foretell that he would face such a miserable situation upon his return?

The chosen people of Jesus' day adhered to Malachi's prophecy that Elijah would come first as a heralder before the Messiah appeared. They were eagerly looking forward to the day when Elijah would descend from the clouds. Meanwhile, an ordinary man of lowly birth, as most of the people viewed Jesus, claimed to be the Messiah even before they had heard any news of Elijah's second coming. As a result, he was mistrusted and ultimately despised and persecuted.

> As Jesus reflected upon his situation, he foresaw that at the Second Advent, the Christians awaiting his return would once more fix their gaze upon the sky. Hence, they would be likely to persecute Christ at the Second Advent if he were born in the flesh and appeared unexpectedly like a thief. They would condemn him as a heretic, just as Jesus was condemned. That is why he foretold that the Lord would suffer and be rejected by his generation. This prophecy can be fulfilled

only if Christ returns in the flesh; it cannot possibly come true if he comes on the clouds. (*Exposition of the Divine Principle,* 385-386)

Jesus also foretold: "Nevertheless when the Son of man cometh, shall he find faith on the earth?" (Luke 18:8). How can Christians fall into faithlessness if the Lord of the Second Advent will show up on the clouds with the loud sounds of angels' trumpets glorifying God? Everyone will be mesmerized and fall into repentance upon seeing this miraculous event. This prophecy also can never be fulfilled if Christ returns in a supernatural manner.

At Jesus' time many Jews kept the prophecy that Elijah would return before the coming of the Messiah. However, Jesus proclaimed that he was the Messiah even before the Jews heard of any news of Elijah's second coming. Therefore, Jesus appeared to be an impostor. He could not find any faithful believer to follow him even to the point of death. Jesus grieved over this situation and lamented that something very similar might happen upon his return, when the believers would be looking only toward the sky, thinking that he would descend on the clouds in glory. When Christ does in fact return to the earth as a man of humble origins, he may not find any faith, as was the case in Jesus' time. Jesus' prediction can only be fulfilled when the returning Christ is born on the earth.

Jesus also foretold: "Many will say to me in that day, Lord, Lord, have we not prophesied in thy name? and in thy name have we cast out devils? and in thy name done many wonderful works? And then will I profess unto them, I never knew you: depart from me, ye that work iniquity" (Matthew 7:22-23). Why would Jesus reject such faithful Christians upon his return? It is because these Christians will reject and persecute Christ at the Second Advent when he returns by being born as a man. Many Christians who are faithful to their own set of doctrines and rituals, would surely serve the Lord of the Second Advent if and when he comes on the clouds in great glory. Naturally, the Lord would then receive them warmly. However, since Jesus prophesied that he would reject them this prophecy also cannot be fulfilled if Jesus comes on the clouds.

In Jesus' time, many Jews were faithful enough that they could even perform miracles in God's name. However, many of them failed to accept him because they were expecting Elijah's return from the clouds. As a result, Jesus had to abandon them in tears.

> In like manner, at the Second Advent of Christ, those Christians who expect his miraculous and glorious appearance will almost certainly reject him if he comes in the flesh of humble birth. No matter how faithful they may be, the Lord will be left with no choice but to abandon them because they will have transgressed against God. (*Exposition of the Divine Principle, 387*)

When Jesus was asked about when the kingdom of God should come, he said that his kingdom is not coming with signs to be observed: "The kingdom of God cometh not with observation" (Luke 17:20). If the Lord of the Second Advent comes on the clouds or in some supernatural way, the kingdom of God will surely arrive with signs of wonder that every person throughout the world would notice.

Jesus said, "The days will come, when ye shall desire to see one of the days of the Son of man, and ye shall not see it" (Luke 17:22). Obviously, everyone will see the Lord if he comes on the clouds with the sounds of angels' trumpets. This verse can only be fulfilled if he comes through birth.

At Christ's' first advent, many religious people could not see the day of the Lord, even though their desire was to see him. Likewise, at the second advent of Christ, many Christians will not be able to see the day because they are already convinced that the Lord will come in a miraculous way.

Since Christ returns through a physical birth, he will appear to be a heretic to Christians who expect him to come on the clouds. Therefore, Jesus warned his followers that if they want to have a spiritual life, they might have to reach beyond their usual comfort zone when it comes to their spiritual beliefs. This is why he said, "Whosoever shall seek to save his life shall lose it; and whosoever shall lose his life shall preserve it" (Luke 17:33).

What, then, is the meaning of the verse that Christ will return on the clouds, considering that his return will take place through his birth here on earth?

> Behold, he cometh with clouds; and every eye shall see him, and they also which pierced him: and all kindreds of the earth shall wail because of him. Even so, Amen. (Revelation 1:7)

The clouds must symbolize something else. In the Bible, water often symbolizes fallen people:

> Send thine hand from above; rid me, and deliver me out of great waters, from the hand of strange children; Whose mouth speaketh vanity, and their right hand is a right hand of falsehood. (Psalm 144:7, 8)

> And he saith unto me, The waters which thou sawest, where the whore sitteth, are peoples, and multitudes, and nations, and tongues. (Revelation 17:15)

Clouds are formed by water being lifted up through evaporation of impure water from the earth. Given this explanation, we can surmise that clouds represent devout Christians whose hearts dwell in heaven and not on the earth because they have been reborn and raised from their fallen state - like 'clouds.'

In another example, The Bible uses the symbolism of clouds to indicate the multitudes:

> Wherefore seeing we also are compassed about with so great a cloud of witnesses, let us lay aside every weight, and the sin which doth so easily beset us, and let us run with patience the race that is set before us. (Hebrews 12:1)

> Thou shalt ascend and come like a storm, thou shalt be like a cloud to cover the land, thou, and all thy bands, and many people with thee. (Ezekiel 38:9)

From this viewpoint, we can conclude that Jesus' coming on the clouds signifies that he will emerge from among a multitude of reborn believers. When Jesus was asked about the place of his return, he replied, "Wheresoever the body is, thither will the eagles be gathered together" (Luke 17:37). Christ is the "body" around whom the "eagles" (his faithful people) will congregate at the resurrection when Christ returns to this world.

When we interpret the clouds metaphorically in this way, Jesus symbolically came down from heaven in the First Advent. Jesus said, "And no man hath ascended up to heaven, but he that came down from heaven, even the Son of man which is in heaven" (John 3:13). Jesus was born on the earth, but from the standpoint of the providence and with regard to his true value, he indeed came from 'heaven'. Thus, the prophet Daniel prophesied that Christ would come on the clouds:

> I saw in the night visions, and, behold, one like the Son of man came with the clouds of heaven, and came to the Ancient of days, and they brought him near before him. (Daniel 7:13)

Contrary to the 'cloud' belief, some Christians believe that Christ's Second Advent occurs simply whenever Jesus comes to dwell within the hearts of people through the descent of the Holy Spirit. However, If this were truly the Second Advent, then it already occurred two thousand years ago, because Jesus has been dwelling within the hearts of faithful believers ever since his resurrection and the Holy Spirit's descent at Pentecost:

> And when the day of Pentecost was fully come, they were all with one accord in one place. And suddenly there came a sound from heaven as of a rushing mighty wind, and it filled all the house where they were sitting. And there appeared unto them cloven tongues like as of fire, and it sat upon each of them. And they were all filled with the Holy Ghost, and began to speak with other tongues, as the Spirit gave them utterance. (Acts 2:1-4)

When Will Christ Come Again?

For most Christians, this question has no answer. In fact, some consider it heresy to pinpoint the exact time of Christ's return. I cannot criticize them because the Bible itself says that no one knows of Christ's return, not even the angels, but the Father Himself alone.

> But of that day and hour knoweth no man, no, not the angels of heaven, but my Father only. (Matthew 24:36)

When will the second coming of Christ happen? According to the verse above, no one knows. However, the Divine Principle explains that we **will come to** know the time of Christ's return. Although the Bible says that no one knows, it also says that God reveals His secrets. Amos 3:7 says, "Surely the Lord God does nothing, without revealing his secret to his servants the prophets." God, who knows the day and hour, will surely reveal all the secrets about the Second Advent to His prophets before He carries out His work.

What about what John says in Revelation 3:3 that Christ will come like a 'thief in the night'? Within that same verse is a warning: "Remember therefore how thou hast received and heard, and hold fast, and repent. If therefore thou shalt not watch, I will come on thee as a thief, and thou shalt not know what hour I will come upon thee." Christ will not come like a thief if we are open to God's present day work in the world.

At the events at Jesus' first coming, he came like a thief to the priests and scribes who were in darkness, but to the family of John the Baptist, who was in the light, God plainly revealed Jesus' birth beforehand. When Jesus was born,

God announced this secret to the three wise men, Simon, Anna, and the shepherds.

Jesus warned us to be careful so that we can be prepared for his return:

> And take heed to yourselves, lest at any time your hearts be overcharged with surfeiting, and drunkenness, and cares of this life, and so that day come upon you unawares. For as a snare shall it come on all them that dwell on the face of the whole earth. Watch ye therefore, and pray always, that ye may be accounted worthy to escape all these things that shall come to pass, and to stand before the Son of man. (Luke 21:34-36)

Jesus taught us that the secret of the time, place, and manner of his return would be revealed to the faithful people who are vigilant and in the light.

So, when will Christ come again? There is a saying that history repeats itself, and it is true. We learn from the Bible that the period from Adam to Abraham was approximately 2,000 years. From Abraham to Jesus was also approximately 2,000 years, and from Jesus to this present age is approximately 2,000 years. These ages display contemporaneously occurring events, and they happened not by accident or without reason.

Parallel incidents have occurred throughout human history. For Unificationists, history is God's story, hence the phrase, "His story." God labored intensely to restore humanity all throughout the history of humankind.

The Divine Principle reveals the exact time of Christ's return, as clearly shown on the following chart:

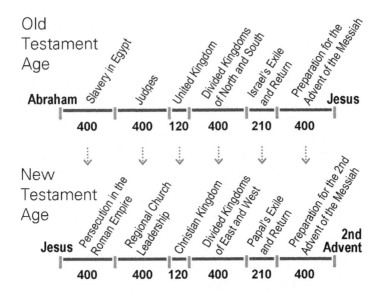

So, what is this chart is telling us? It describes in detail God's work of salvation or "restoration." Let's examine each of its providential restoration periods.

The Period of Slavery in Egypt and the Period of Persecution in the Roman Empire

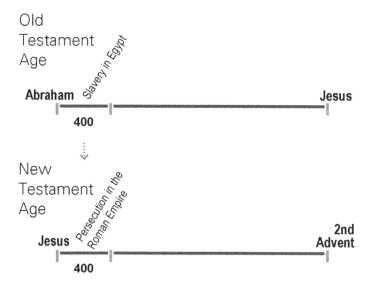

One can see a stunning similarity of events beginning with the Old Testament Age from Abraham to Jesus and then beginning anew with the New Testament Age from Jesus to the present day. During the Old Testament Age, the Israelites underwent a 400-year period of slavery in Egypt until Moses' era. Likewise, during the New Testament Age, early Christians had undergone a 400-year period of persecution in the Roman Empire.

The Period of the Judges and the Period of Regional Church Leadership

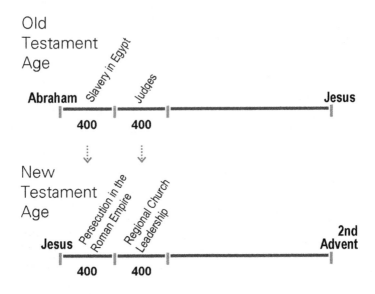

The next 400 years, after Moses, was the Period of the Judges. The judges governed the tribes of Israel. The judges performed the roles of prophet, priest, and king, which became separate offices in the later periods. Israel in this period was a feudalistic society with no central political authority.

Similarly, in the New Testament Age, the next 400 years was the Period of Regional Church Leadership. During this period, regional church leaders—patriarchs, bishops, and abbots—led Christian society. Like the judges of the Old Testament Age, they had duties similar to those of prophet, priest, and king. As in the time of the Judges, Christian culture in this period was part of a feudalistic society under these local authorities.

The Period of the United Kingdom and the Period of the Christian Empire

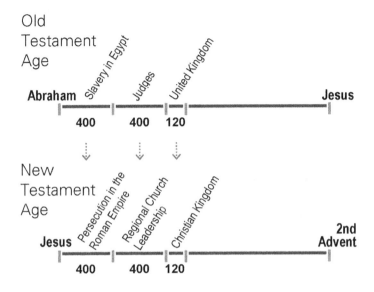

Finally, the age of the Judges ended, followed by the 120-year Period of the United Kingdom. When Israel first entered the period of the United Kingdom, the role of the judges was to serve either as a prophet, priest, or a king. The prophets received instructions directly from God, the priests kept charge over the Tabernacle and later the Temple, and the king governed the nation. Each carried on his distinct missions in guiding Israel to accomplish the goal of the providence of restoration.

Fast forward to the Christian era when the age of regional church leadership ended, followed by 120-year Period of the Christian Empire. The purpose of this period was to restore the United Kingdom. Thus, when the Period of Regional Church Leadership ended, the missions of these leaders were to be monastic leaders corresponding to the prophets, the pope corresponding to the high priest, and the emperor, to the king who ruled the people. Just as the Judges of the Old Testament Age were responsible to guide Israel, the Christian church leaders were responsible to guide Christianity as the Second Israel to accomplish the goal of the providence of restoration.

King Saul was anointed by the prophet Samuel as the first king of Israel (1 Samuel 8:19-22; 10:1-24). He was in the position to restore the four hundred years of slavery in Egypt and Moses' forty years in the Pharaoh's palace by completing the forty years of his reign in accordance with God's desires. However, because King Saul disobeyed the commands of God given through the prophet Samuel (1 Samuel 15:1-23), he was in no position to build the Temple.

Consequently, the providence of restoration through King Saul was extended. Forty years of King David's reign and forty years of King Solomon's reign would pass before the foundation of faith was laid and the Temple was built.

King Solomon fell into lust with his many foreign wives, who turned him away from God (1 Kings 11:3-7). Hence, there was no way for Israel to establish the foundation for the Messiah, which should have been laid in the period of the United Kingdom.

Likewise, in the New Testament era, Pope Leo III crowned Charlemagne and blessed him as the first emperor of Christendom in 800 A.D. Charlemagne stood upon the foundation of the 400-year period of regional church leadership. By faithfully living according to the teachings of Jesus in his work to realize the Christian ideal of the state, he was to establish the foundation of faith. Indeed, when Charlemagne was crowned emperor, he achieved this foundation. However, subsequent emperors did not remain obedient to God's will, and the foundation for the Second Advent of the Messiah was not established during that time.

The Period of the Divided Kingdoms of North and South and the Period of the Divided Kingdoms of East and West

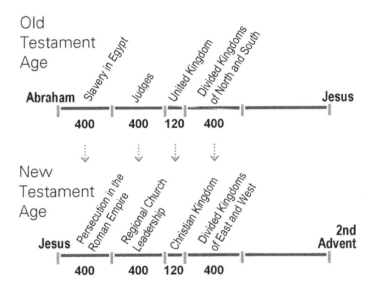

Following the 120-year Period of the United Kingdom was the 400-year Period of the Divided Kingdoms of North and South. During this time, King Solomon failed to follow God's will. He was led by his many wives and concubines to worship idols. As a result, having lasted only three generations, the United Kingdom of Israel was divided upon his death: the kingdom of Israel in the north, which was founded by ten of the twelve tribes, and the kingdom of Judah in the south, which was founded by the two remaining tribes.

This was how the Period of the Divided Kingdoms of North and South began.

Similarly, following the 120-year Period of the Christian Empire was the Period of the Divided Kingdoms of East and West. Charlemagne's grandsons partitioned the Christian empire into three kingdoms: the East Franks, the West Franks, and Italy. This division also began in the third generation. The descendants of Charlemagne were in bitter and constant conflict with each other. The remnants of the Christian empire soon coalesced into two kingdoms, with Italy reverting to the rule of the East Franks. The kingdom of the East Franks came to be called the Holy Roman Empire.

During the Old Testament Age, whenever the Israelites violated their covenant with God, straying from the ideal of the Temple, God sent many prophets, such as Elijah, Isaiah, and Jeremiah, to admonish them and inspire them to repentance and internal reform. However, because the kings and the people did not heed the warnings of the prophets and did not repent, God chastised them externally by sending Gentile nations such as Syria, Assyria, and Babylon to attack them.

During Christian times when the church leadership turned away from God's will, God sent prominent monks such as St. Thomas Aquinas and St. Francis of Assisi to admonish the papacy and promote internal reform within the Church. However, the church did not repent and sank even further into corruption. God chastised them by letting their people fight the Muslims. This was the providential reason behind the Crusades.

The Period of the Divided Kingdoms of North and South ended when the people of Israel and Judah were taken into exile by the Gentile nations, which also ended the monarchy in Israel. Similarly, at the end of the Period of the Divided Kingdoms of East and West, the papacy had suffered repeated defeats in the Crusades, which completely lost its prestige and credibility. As a result, Christianity lost its center of spiritual sovereignty. Feudal society lost its political power and vigor and eventually eroded monarchic Christianity.

The Period of Israel's Exile and Return and the Period of the Papal Exile and Return

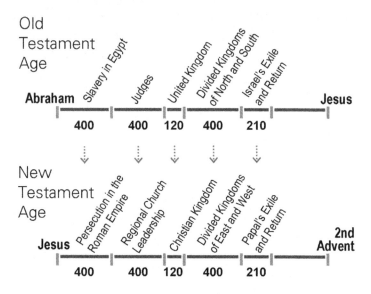

During the Old Testament Age, the people of Israel failed to establish God's nation founded upon the Temple. They fell into faithlessness without repentance. As a result, their people suffered hardships as exiles in Babylon. This was similar to when God had the Israelites suffer as slaves in Egypt.

Nearly seventy years elapsed from the time King Nebuchadnezzar of Babylon took into captivity King Jehoiachin and his royal family, as well as prophets, priests, officials, craftsmen, and many other Israelites, until they were liberated by the royal decree of King Cyrus, when Babylon fell. It took the Israelites another one hundred and forty years for the exiles to return to their homeland in three waves until they fully reformed themselves as a nation united around the will of God as proclaimed in the Messianic prophecies of

Malachi. From this time, they began to prepare for the coming of the Messiah.

Strikingly, during the New Testament Age, God's intention for the Christian empire was that ultimately it would bequeath the empire and the throne to the Lord of the Second Advent when he would come as the King of kings and build God's kingdom on earth. However, the emperors and popes became corrupt and were unable to lay the foundation for the Second Advent of Christ. To begin a new dispensation to restore this foundation, God allowed the popes to be taken into exile and suffer captivity.

The papacy lost the confidence of the people. Its authority sank even lower because of repeated defeats during the Crusades. The conflict between the popes and the kings escalated. In one such conflict, King Philip IV "the Fair" of France, imprisoned Pope Boniface VIII. In 1309, the king forced Pope Clement V to move the papacy from Rome to Avignon in southern France. For seventy years, successive popes lived there, subject to the kings of France, until Pope Gregory XI returned the papal residence to Rome in the year 1377.

After Pope Gregory XI died, papal rivalry occurred. The Cardinals elected Pope Urban VI, an Italian, as the new pope. However, he was rejected by another group of cardinals, mostly Frenchmen, who then elected another pope, Clement VII. This created a rival papacy in Avignon. The Great Schism continued into the next century. In an effort to resolve this conflict, in the year 1409, the Cardinals from both camps held a council in Pisa, Italy. The council dismissed both the Roman and Avignon popes and appointed Alexander V as the legitimate pope. However, the two popes refused to resign, creating a spectacle of three contending popes. Following that, cardinals, bishops, theologians, royalty, and their envoys gathered for the General Council of Constance (1414-1417), which dismissed all three popes and elected Martin V as the new pope. This ended the Great Schism.

This time period took approximately two hundred and ten years from the year 1309 in the period of Papal Exile and Return, starting with the papacy's seventy years of exile in Avignon and extending through the Great Schism, the conciliar movement, and the restoration of papal authority in the Roman church to the eve of the Protestant Reformation spearheaded by Martin Luther in the year 1517. These events were subsequently parallel to the period of Israel's Exile and Return during the Old Testament Age. Its purpose was to restore the 210-year period from Israel's seventy years of exile in Babylon through the stages of the returning to Israel and the rebuilding of the Temple, until the reform of politics and religion under the leadership of Ezra, Nehemiah, and the prophet Malachi.

The Period of Preparation for the Advent of the Messiah and the Period of Preparation for the Second Advent of the Messiah

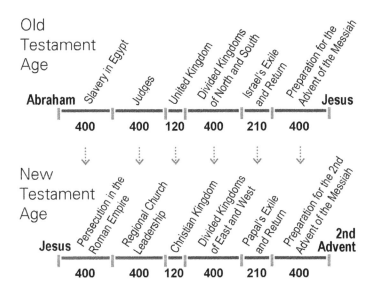

Following the Period of Israel's Exile and Return before Jesus Christ came was a 400-year period—the Period of Preparation for the Advent of the Messiah. Similarly, following the Period of Papal Exile and Return was a 400-year Period of Preparation for the *Second* Advent of the Messiah. Christianity is to meet the Lord of the Second Advent only after passing through this 400-year period.

To prepare humanity for the First Coming of Christ, God sent the prophet Malachi to the chosen people four hundred and thirty years in advance to kindle in them a strong Messianic expectation. Also, God encouraged the Jews to reform their religion and deepen their faith to make the internal preparations necessary to receive the Messiah.

The Divine Principle says:

Meanwhile, among the world's peoples, God founded religions suited to their regions and cultures by which they could make the necessary internal preparations to receive the Messiah. In India, God established Buddhism through Gautama Buddha (565-485 B.C.) as a new development out of Hinduism. In Greece, God inspired Socrates (470-399 B.C.) and opened the brilliant age of classical Greek civilization. In the Far East, God raised up Confucius (552-479 B.C.), whose teachings of Confucianism established the standard of human ethics. Jesus was to come upon this worldwide foundation of preparation, and through his teachings, he was to bring together Judaism, Hellenism, Buddhism and Confucianism. He was to unify all religions and civilizations into one worldwide civilization founded upon the Christian Gospel.

Since the Renaissance, God has been creating the religious, political, and economic environment conducive to the work of Christ at his Second Coming. This has been the age to restore through indemnity, in the form of substantial parallels, the earlier period when God had set up the worldwide environment to prepare for the coming of Jesus. Beginning with the Renaissance, progress in virtually every field of human endeavor, including politics, economy, culture, and science, has increased at a rapid rate. Today, these fields have reached their zenith and have created a global environment conducive to the work of Christ at his Second Coming. In Jesus' day, the Roman Empire ruled the vast domains around the Mediterranean Sea, integrated by an advanced and extensive transportation system reaching out in all directions. This was the center of a vast Hellenistic civilization founded on the Greek language. Thus, all the necessary preparations had been made for a swift transmission of the teachings of the Messiah from Israel, where Jesus lived, to Rome and the world. Similarly, in the present era of the Second Advent, the influence of the Western powers has expanded the democratic political sphere throughout the world. The rapid progress of transportation and communication has greatly bridged the gap between East and West, and the extensive contact among languages and cultures has brought the world much closer together. These factors have fully prepared an environment in which the teachings of the returning Christ can freely and swiftly be conveyed to the hearts of all humankind. This will enable his teachings to bring rapid and profound changes all over the globe. (*Exposition of the Divine Principle*, 327-328)

In reference to the previous chart, let's calculate the number of years:

Abraham to Jesus (Old Testament Age):
400+400+120+400+210+400=1,930
Jesus to the present era (New Testament Age):
400+400+120+400+210+400=1,930

Both Ages have roughly 2,000 years each; therefore, they could be referred to as 2,000-year periods.

One thousand nine hundred and thirty years separate Abraham and Jesus. Not coincidentally, the total number of years from Jesus to the Second Advent is also 1,930.

Astonishingly, what this calculation indicates is that the time of Christ's return should occur in the year 1930. Then, is 1930 the precise year the Messiah was born? The year cannot be pinpointed very exactly because a difference of up to ten years has often occurred throughout the providential history. For example, the 400-year Period of the Persecution in the Roman Empire lasted only for three hundred and ninety two years (0-392 A.D.). The 400-year Period of Preparation for the Second Coming began with the Reformation in 1517 and ended four hundred years later. Based on this, the Second Coming should have occurred in 1917. Thus, the birth of the anointed one, or the Second Advent, should have taken place some time between 1917 and 1930.

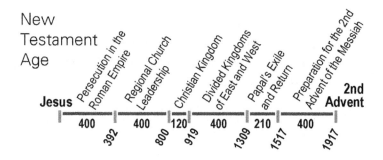

Clearly, the evidence demonstrates that the present days *are* the Last Days and Christ has returned! The Divine Principle says:

> We call the time of Christ's Second Advent the Last Days, and we are living in the Last Days today. We can thus understand that today is truly the time of Christ's return. From the standpoint of providential history, Jesus came at the conclusion of the two-thousand-year-long Old Testament Age, the Age of the Providence of Restoration. The Principle of Restoration through Indemnity leads us to infer that Christ is to return at the

end of the two-thousand-year-long New Testament Age. (*Exposition of the Divine Principle*, 382)

However, as I mentioned earlier, the earth will not literally end despite the dire predictions. Rather the 'Last Days' is the end of the old era and the present days are the beginning of the new era. The Lord of the Second Advent already proclaimed the era of the Completed Testament which will out shine the New Testament Age just as the New Testament Age outshone the Old Testament Age when Christ brought the Gospel into the world. The Lord of the Second Advent brings a new expression of truth and proclaims the Completed Testament Age, thus fulfilling what Jesus promised in John 16:25 that he will reveal a deeper understanding about the will of God.

As I've mentioned in the beginning of this book, no one knows of Christ's return. However, for those who are awake, who live in the light, surely the Father will reveal His plans. I strongly recommend that you pray to God about this content.

If you want to read and learn more about this, please visit www.DiscoverDP.info to purchase *Exposition of the Divine Principle*. Then, come to one of our Divine Principle lectures at your local Unification Church.

Why Christ Must Come Again

So, what is the purpose of the Messiah's return? To answer this question, we need to understand why the Messiah, Jesus Christ, came. Jesus came to fulfill God's work of salvation. What do we have to be saved from? Human beings need salvation because of the Fall of our first human ancestors, Adam and Eve.

What was the Fall? Adam and Eve disobeyed God's commandment not to eat the fruit of the Tree of the Knowledge of Good and Evil. But, because of their disobedience, they failed to embody God's given blessing, mentioned in Genesis 1:28:

> And God blessed them, and God said unto them, Be fruitful, and multiply, and replenish the earth, and subdue it: and have dominion over the fish of the sea, and over the fowl of the air, and over every living thing that moveth upon the earth.

What is the significance of this verse? The Divine Principle refers to this as "**The Three Great Blessings**":

1st **Be fruitful**

2nd **Multiply**

3rd **Have dominion**

The Divine Principle refers to these three blessings as instructions for Adam and Eve, and for humanity, to live in accordance with the will of God (which means to do good). Adam and Eve were to be fruitful, which means to mature in character and in love, thereby becoming an ideal husband and an ideal wife. Unfortunately, before they reached maturity, they were tempted by the Archangel to engage in a sexual relationship. They could not reach maturity so that God could bless them in an eternal relationship of marriage. Thus, they became a fallen husband and a fallen wife. If Adam and Eve had reached maturity, they would have fulfilled the second blessing, which was to multiply children of goodness. Instead, their act of false love cost them their lineage which then led them to multiply children outside the dominion of God.

If Adam and Eve fulfilled the first and second blessing, they would have achieved a loving dominion over all of creation including the earth, animals and even the cosmos, thus creating an environment not only conducive to humanity's needs but one in which the earth would not be abused. Unfortunately, because of the Fall, all creation suffered under false masters. Romans 8:19 says, "For the earnest expectation of the creature waiteth for the manifestation of the sons of God."

Because of the Fall, humanity lost its lineage from God-centered to Satan-centered. This is the reason Jesus said, "You are of your father the devil" (John 8:48, Matthew 23:32). Jesus refers to the people as "snakes" and "a brood of vipers."

Jesus, the son of God, came to earth to fulfill the Three Great Blessings. He came with the seed of God's lineage. He was born without the original sin. Although he was able to attain the first blessing, unfortunately, he was not able to find a bride because he was killed. His lineage was cut off, and God's purpose of creation was left undone. This is the very reason why the Messiah, the Lord of the Second Advent, has to come again.

The Messiah must come again to fulfill the Three Great Blessings, the fulfillment of God's purpose of creation. The Messiah will stand as the restored Adam, the bridegroom. He will raise an ideal bride, the restored Eve. Hence, the Bible mentions that the marriage of the Lamb shall take place in the Last Days:

> Let us be glad and rejoice, and give honour to him: for the marriage of the Lamb is come, and his wife hath made herself ready. (Revelation 19:7)

Adam and Eve consummated their love relationship outside of God's realm and they became false parents. Satan became the ancestor of humankind (John 8:44). The Messiah and his bride, the restored Adam and restored Eve, will stand as the True Parents of humanity. These two individuals, uniting as one, will be the living embodiments of God on earth as the Heavenly Parent.

Humanity's ultimate salvation comes only when we are reborn in the realm of the True Parents. For humanity to be saved, we need to be adopted by the True Parents:

> And not only they, but ourselves also, which have the first fruits of the Spirit, even we ourselves groan within ourselves, waiting for the adoption, to wit, the redemption of our body. (Romans 8:23)

Every individual must be reborn to receive salvation, but we cannot be reborn through one person alone. We need Christ and his bride, the restored Eve, both standing as the True Father and the True Mother of humanity.

And I saw a new heaven and a new earth: for the first heaven and the first earth were passed away; and there was no more sea. (Revelation 21:1)

The new world that the True Parents will establish is a world of peace, harmony, and prosperity. God's purpose of creation is to establish the kingdom of heaven on earth. On this foundation, the kingdom of heaven in the spirit world will also be established. This has been Jesus' earnest desire:

Our Father which art in heaven, Hallowed be thy name. Thy kingdom come, Thy will be done in earth, as it is in heaven. (Matthew 6:9-10)

The new expression of truth will finally unlock all the secrets of the Bible and reveal to us the heart of God. Thus, Jesus said:

I have yet many things to say unto you, but ye cannot bear them now. Howbeit when he, the Spirit of truth, is come, he will guide you into all truth: for he shall not speak of himself; but whatsoever he shall hear, that shall he speak: and he will shew you things to come. He shall glorify me: for he shall receive of mine, and shall shew it unto you. (John 16:12-14)

Jesus also said:

These things have I spoken unto you in proverbs: but the time cometh, when I shall no more speak unto you in proverbs, but I shall shew you plainly of the Father. (John 16:25)

With this new expression of truth, humanity will enter the Completed Testament era. God says in Acts 2:17-18 that in the last days, "I will pour out my Spirit on all people. Your sons and daughters will prophesy, your young men will see visions, your old men will dream dreams. Even on my servants, both men and women, I will pour out my Spirit in those days, and they will prophesy." And, with this truth, we are told that we "must prophesy again about many peoples, nations, languages and kings" (Revelation 10:10) in order for this truth to be taught in all corners of the world.

The new expression of truth must resolve the disparity between science and religion. But most importantly, humanity's fallen lineage must be engrafted back to God's lineage, which will allow God to substantially dwell on earth. This is how the kingdom of heaven on earth will be established. So, although it is a time of tumult it is also a time of great hope!

Where Will Christ Return?

If Christ, in fact, comes again as a man born on the earth, then where would that be? Where is the place God has chosen for Christ's return? Who would be the people chosen to receive him? He will certainly be born among a people who are chosen by God.

Many Christians expect that Christ will come again among the Jewish people, based on this passage from the Bible:

> And I heard the number of them which were sealed: and there were sealed an hundred and forty and four thousand of all the tribes of the children of Israel. (Revelation 7:4)

However, to interpret this verse literally will lead to misunderstanding God's providence. On this matter, Jesus uttered the parable of the vineyard:

> Hear another parable: There was a certain householder, which planted a vineyard, and hedged it round about, and digged a winepress in it, and built a tower, and let it out to husbandmen, and went into a far country: And when the time of the fruit drew near, he sent his servants to the husbandmen, that they might receive the fruits of it. And the husbandmen took his servants, and beat one, and killed another, and stoned another. Again, he sent other servants more than the first: and they did unto them likewise. But last of all he sent unto them his son, saying, They will reverence my son. But when the husbandmen saw the son, they said among themselves, This is the heir; come, let us kill

him, and let us seize on his inheritance. And they caught him, and cast him out of the vineyard, and slew him. When the lord therefore of the vineyard cometh, what will he do unto those husbandmen? They say unto him, He will miserably destroy those wicked men, and will let out his vineyard unto other husbandmen, which shall render him the fruits in their seasons. Jesus saith unto them, Did ye never read in the scriptures, The stone which the builders rejected, the same is become the head of the corner: this is the Lord's doing, and it is marvelous in our eyes? Therefore say I unto you, The kingdom of God shall be taken from you, and given to a nation bringing forth the fruits thereof. (Matthew 21:33-43)

Jesus used this parable to explain that Christ will not return among the Jewish people.

Christ will Not Return Among the Jewish People

Christ will not come again among the Jewish people who rejected him. The Divine Principle explains:

In this parable, the householder represents God, the vineyard represents God's work, the tenants entrusted with the work represent the Jewish people, the servants represent the prophets, the son of the householder represents Jesus, and the other tenants who harvest the fruits represent some other nation which can receive Christ at the Second Advent and realize God's Will. By this parable, Jesus conveyed that he would not come again to the people who persecuted him. God will take away the mission previously entrusted to them and give it to another people who can produce its fruits upon Christ's return." (*Exposition of the Divine Principle, 396-397*)

Then why is it that, according to Revelation 7:4, Christ will come again from Israel? The word "Israel" means "the one who has prevailed." Genesis 32:28 tells us that Jacob received the name Israel upon his victory against the angel who wrestled with him at the ford of Jabbok. "And he said, Thy name shall be called no more Jacob, but Israel: for as a prince hast thou power with God and with men, and hast prevailed." His victory was a condition for his descendants to lay a foundation to receive the Messiah. From this victorious condition, Jacob's descendants were called *Israel*, or the chosen people. The term "Israel" therefore signifies the people of God who have triumphed through their faith. It does not, however, necessarily apply to everyone who comes out of Jacob's lineage alone. This is the reason why John the Baptist said in Matthew 3:9, "And think not to say within yourselves, We have Abraham to our father: for I say unto you, that God is able of these stones to raise up children unto Abraham." St. Paul conveyed his message to Christians in Rome that not all who are descended from Israel are Israel (Romans 9:6).

The new chosen people, or the second Israel, are the Christians. The Divine Principle says:

> Who became the chosen people after Jesus' crucifixion? They were none other than the Christians who inherited the faith of Abraham and took on the mission which Abraham's descendants did not complete. St. Paul wrote, "Through their trespass salvation has come to the Gentiles, so as to make Israel jealous"

103

(Romans 11:11), testifying that the center of God's providence of restoration had shifted from the Jews to the Gentiles (Acts 13:46). Therefore, the chosen people who should lay the foundation for Christ at the Second Advent are not the descendants of Abraham, but rather the Christians who have inherited the faith of Abraham. (*Exposition of the Divine Principle, 398*)

If Christ will not return in the nation of Israel, where will he return? Christ will return to a nation in the East. Revelation 5:5 tells us of the Lion of the tribe of Judah, the Root of David, "hath prevailed to open the book, and to loose the seven seals." The Lion signifies Christ, who will open the seven seals in the Last Days. After six of the seals are opened:

> And I saw another angel ascending from the east, having the seal of the living God: and he cried with a loud voice to the four angels, to whom it was given to hurt the earth and the sea, Saying, Hurt not the earth, neither the sea, nor the trees, till we have sealed the servants of our God in their foreheads. (Revelation 7:2-3)

The nation that will inherit the work of God and bear its fruit for the sake of the Second Advent is in the East. There, Christ will be born and received by the chosen people of God. Which among the nations of the East is chosen to receive the Lord? The Nation in the East is Korea. The Divine Principle says:

> Since ancient times, the nations in the East have traditionally been considered the three nations of Korea, Japan, and China. Among them, Japan throughout its history has worshipped the sun goddess, Amaterasu-omi-kami. Japan entered the period of the

Second Advent as a fascist nation and severely persecuted Korean Christianity. China at the time of the Second Advent was a hotbed of communism and would become a communist nation. Thus, God could not send His son to these nations. Korea, then, is the nation in the East where Christ will return. (*Exposition of the Divine Principle, 399*)

The *Exposition of the Divine Principle* explains at great length how Korea meets the qualifications to be the birthplace for the Messiah. A study of its unique culture, history and heritage can attest to that upon further study.

Is the Reverend Sun Myung Moon the Messiah?

First, I would like to say that this question, whether Sun Myung Moon is the messiah or not, is *not* discussed in the *Exposition of the Divine Principle.*

Is Reverend Moon the one that we are waiting for? It all depends on how you define the word, "Messiah." If you believe that the Messiah will literally descend to earth from the clouds, as a fantastical being surrounded by platoons of angels blowing their trumpets, when the dead people will literally rise up from their graves, and we who are alive will be literally caught up on the clouds, then, definitely, Reverend Moon is not the one. However, if you believe that Christ's return will be manifested through another person born on earth, then this makes sense that Unificationists believe that Reverend Moon is the one.

When I give lectures about the Second Coming, people asked me, "Where would Jesus be in this equation?" Jesus will be working with this anointed person to carry out his mission. That anointed person is the returning Christ.

Of course, you are well aware that the word "Christ" is not Jesus' last name. Christ or "Christos" in Greek means, "the anointed one."

On April 17, 1935, the young Sun Myung Moon had a deep encounter with Jesus. In his autobiography, *As A Peace-Loving Global Citizen*, the Reverend Sun Myung Moon wrote:

> *It was the night before Easter in the year I turned six-*
> *teen. I was on Mount Myodu praying all night and beg-*
> *ging God in tears for answers. Why had He created a*
> *world so filled with sorrow and despair? Why was the*

all-knowing and all-powerful God leaving the world in such pain? What should I do for my tragic homeland? I wept in tears as I asked these questions repeatedly. Early Easter morning after I had spent the entire night in prayer, Jesus appeared before me. He appeared in an instant, like a gust of wind, and said to me, "God is in great sorrow because of the pain of humankind. You must take on a special mission on earth having to do with Heaven's work."

That morning, I saw clearly the sorrowful face of Jesus. I heard his voice clearly. The experience of witnessing the manifestation of Jesus caused my body to shake violently, like a quaking aspen's leaves trembling in a strong breeze. I was simultaneously overcome with fear so great I felt I might die and gratitude so profound I felt I might explode. Jesus spoke clearly about the work I would have to do. His words were extraordinary, having to do with saving humanity from its suffering and bringing joy to God. (49-50)

A Divine Principle lecturer said:

From that point, the young man dedicated himself to the task Jesus gave him. Reverend Moon has often been misunderstood. He has been unjustly imprisoned six times for his uncompromising commitment to live by his conscience. But, despite the persecution and torture, he never gave up on this mission that was given to him by God and Jesus Christ.

In 1960, he married Hak Ja Han, and since then they have led their church and movement as co-equal partners. It is a couple-ministry. Reverend Moon ascended to God in

September of 2012, but his ministry continues through his wife, his family and couples in ministry around the world.

You may ask, why would God speak to a farm boy from Korea? Why didn't God speak to someone else? I don't know ultimately. You would have to ask God that question. But I would make a guess. Reverend Moon is a special person. When he was young he came to know that God, as our Heavenly Parent is intensely suffering. Imagine how a parent would feel if their children were killing each other and doing other terrible evil things to each other. Therefore, he prayed, asking what he could do to alleviate God's suffering, what could he do with his life in order to comfort God's heart. As a parent, I would be moved if I heard such a prayer. I would be touched by that and I think God was deeply touched.

Early in his ministry, he put together what he understood from nature, from the Bible and from Jesus and God, into a book called, Exposition of the Divine Principle. It presents the internal principles that enable us to achieve the ideal of creation and to understand the heart of God.

I believe, Reverend Sun Myung Moon is the person anointed by God to succeed Jesus in fulfilling God's purpose of creation. He and his wife, Hak Ja Han, are standing as the True Parents of humanity. Therefore, Unificationists call him the "True Father" and call her the "True Mother."

I don't think that I could explain fully from this book why I believe that Reverend Moon is the Messiah. A profound insight like that takes a lot of prayer and effort to understand. However, from the Unificationist standpoint, Reverend Sun Myung Moon is the one.

However, most Unificationists do not place an overtly high emphasis on Reverend Moon's messiahship. Instead we understand that because of the concept of personal responsibility we all have a duty to practice 'tribal messiahship' in order to help our hurting world. I have been in the Unification Church for over twenty-six years, but I do not remember, or perhaps I never heard, when someone said, "The Messiah is here," when Reverend Moon came to our church centers to meet with us. Instead, we normally say something like, "True Father is here." Personally and up close we witnessed his love for us as he spoke for hours on end, went fishing with members, and treated us like his own children. Like myself, many Unificationists are not bothered with the controversial question of whether Rev. Moon is the Messiah or not, but we all agree that he and his wife stand in the position of True Parents fulfilling the calling of this age; it is their leadership that the world needs now.

If you want to read more about their legacy, please visit my website at www.discoverdp.info/founders.html.

About the Unification Church's Mass Wedding

In the beginning of this book, I mentioned that you've probably wondered why a Unificationist would choose to be married in a mass wedding, A majority of Unificationists, if not all, share the same reasoning, so I think the easiest way to explain this is to share my own testimony.

Since 1988 when I first heard the Divine Principle, my life has not been the same. A few years after my joining, I decided to commit my time to this new ideology and became a missionary of the church. I understood that Reverend and Mrs. Moon were guided by God and Jesus to stand as the True Parents of humankind, and therefore, I trusted them in choosing my future spouse. In July of 1992 my wife and I were paired by True Parents as husband and wife through the Unification Church marriage "matching ceremony." In August of 1992 my wife and I decided to take the next step by participating in the Blessing Ceremony in Seoul, Korea officiated by them personally.

I committed to the Blessing Ceremony - as we call it - because of its providential significance. The purpose of the marriage ceremony of the Unification Church is not the same as a conventional marriage ceremony. It has its unique value. As I mentioned earlier, the Divine Principle explains that Adam and Eve became husband and wife outside the realm of God's dominion because of the Fall. As a result, they lost God's lineage to Satan. This fallen lineage was passed on to all their descendants until today, and this is how evil and conflict continue to multiply.

Jesus came to restore what Adam and Eve lost. However, because of the failure of the people to recognize him as the Messiah, he was not able to fulfill his ultimate goal. He and his would-be bride would have stood in the position as the True Parents of humankind, restoring humanity's lineage by creating the new and vital connection to God.

What then would be the process to restore humanity's lineage back to God? The marriage ceremony of the Unification Church is a "Blessing Ceremony" whereby participants are given the blessing to consummate their conjugal relationship and establish a God-centered family. A most significant part of the Blessing Ceremony is the drinking of the "holy wine" which symbolizes the inheritance of the blood lineage of God. In the New Testament, Jesus performed this ritual during the "Lord's Supper," (Matthew 26:27, 28) but the Blessing Ceremony is at a higher dimension because it has the presence of a complete set of True Parents. This is what Rev. Moon has said about the significance of the blessing:

> *The International Holy Blessing Ceremony is the ceremony of resurrection that enables us to uproot and restore completely all that was defiled in our families because of the Fall, especially the false love, false life and false lineage we received from the false parents... Through the Blessing Ceremony we receive the enormous grace of being engrafted with the seeds of true love, true life and true lineage, by which God and human beings can become one through love. I sincerely hope that all humanity throughout the world will receive this enormous blessing, change to become heavenly families, and be registered in the Kingdom of Heaven on earth. (October 31, 1995)*

Some Unificationists participated in a mass wedding with less attention given to its theological significance, but more because of their sincere devotion to God and to the ideal. Some couples have also joined in because of the vision that the ceremony represents. Generally, Unificationists commit to the Blessing Ceremony with the intention of making this world a better place to live, a world where all nations and races can harmonize as one family.

Unificationists born within the church - in other words, the offspring of parents who attended the Blessing Ceremony - are often given the moniker, "second, third, and fourth gen." The young people in our church may have slightly different reasons for attending the Blessing Ceremony from making a sincere commitment to putting true love at the center of their marriage to carrying on their parent's legacy. Many choose to either precede or follow-up the church's marriage blessing with their own private wedding.

I asked a twenty-four-year-old second generation Unificationist in Seattle, Washington, why he joined the Blessing Ceremony that was held in South Korea in 2013. This is what he wrote to me:

Hey Nelson,

There are many reasons why receiving the Blessing was important to me. The Blessing is given by God through True Parents and I feel that it represents God's acceptance of the relationship. Getting matched, engaged, and married are all the same commitment I made to the one I love, but the Blessing was unique in that I was making that commitment to my wife in front of True Parents while also committing to putting them and God in the center of our relationship. The connection to the worldwide Unification movement also really attracted me to the Blessing. At the Blessing ceremony there were amazing, dedicated people from across the world and we all stood side by side and committed ourselves and our relationships to God. Being in that environment of such faith and love was a powerful and memorable experience. Apart from the faithful aspects of the Blessing, it was important for me to receive it in Korea because that is how my parents committed themselves to one another over 30 years ago. I wanted to be able to carry on the tradition of the Blessing that my parents passed down to me and to experience what they may have experienced.

Whatever the reason they may have for entrusting their fate to the matching process, all Unificationists understand that the foundation to establish a God-centered society starts within a family. The family is "the school of love" and the Blessing Ceremony provides the singular opportunity to begin building that foundation.

Furthermore, the Unification Church marriage has the potential to heal the animosities between nations and races. Rev. and Mrs. Moon matched "blessing candidates" from different nationalities and races in order to achieve this goal. As you may or may not be aware of, the nations of Korea and Japan have had a long history of bitter conflicts. Thousands of Koreans Unificationists were paired with Japanese Unificationists, resolving the historical enmity of "enemy nations" through establishing loving relationship between husbands and wives. In his autobiography book, Rev. Moon explains:

International and intercultural marriages are the quickest way to bring about an ideal world of peace. Things that would take seemingly forever can be accomplished like miracles through these types of marriages in just two or three generations. People should marry across national and cultural boundaries with people from countries they consider to be their enemies so that the world of peace can come that much more quickly. A person may hate people from a certain country or culture and think he never wants to set eyes on them. But if someone from that country becomes his spouse, then the person is halfway to becoming a person of the new country. All the hatred melts away. If this is repeated for two or three generations, the roots of hatred can be eliminated.

White and black people will marry each other; Japanese will marry Koreans and people from Africa. Many millions are entering into such international and intercultural marriages. A completely new lineage is being created as a result. A new kind of human being that transcends white, black, and yellow is being born. I am not just referring to marriages across international boundaries. The same is true for marrying people from other religions or denominations. In fact, marriages between people of different religions are even more difficult than international marriages. Even if two religious groups have been fighting each other for centuries, it is possible to bring harmony between them by having their followers marry each other. In such a marriage, one spouse will not close himself off from the other just because she was raised in a different tradition.

(As A Peace-Loving Global Citizen; 218-219; The Washington Times Foundation; Copyright 2011)

Can non-Unificationists participate in the Blessing Ceremony? The answer is *yes*, though of course, it is more meaningful if one understands and accepts it significance. God's blessing is for everyone. Is the Blessing Ceremony only for unmarried people? The answer is *no*. Married couples can join in. Thousands of married couples have already participated in the ceremony as a wonderful way to renew their vows.

About a decade ago I watched the news on television of our Blessing Ceremony. The media showed married couples' faces exhausted at the events, dubbed it with eerie soundtracks - and voila! - they had scintillating news coverage slapped with the ominous lead, "Cult Wedding." We were portrayed as people who didn't know any better. I was thinking, "My goodness, give us a break, these people are getting married! Even a little bit of congratulations would be greatly appreciated rather than mockery. These participants are making their own choices, and they are having so much fun!"

Did I mention that Unificationists who attended the Blessing Ceremony are making their own choices? Yes, they are! Even though many of the couples were matched, each person has to decide whether or not to accept his or her partner. The Blessing Ceremony does not happen overnight. In the early days of our movement there were many Unificationists who went to the Blessing Ceremony only after a three year engagement period. Why? It is because they wanted to invest effort to build a foundation to become better husbands and better wives. Of course, there are those who met each other only few days before the Blessing event and based on their faith they forged ahead. Talk about faith! And a willingness to love whoever God gives you.

To enter into the marriage matching process requires some investment. A matching applicant needs to ensure that he or she has a healthy spiritual, physical, and mental life. Each person goes through a series of talks on Blessing Education which, like any church program, includes advice for young couples.

Some of our detractors have been fascinated by the idea that after the Blessing Ceremony, couples have to separate for forty days before having sex. I guess it is normal to be curious about members of a religious group's sexual lives! In our church we call this "40-Day Separation Period," but couples are not really separated. Instead, their acquaintance and communication develops. I prefer calling it a "40-Day Preparation Period." My wife and I had only met in person for the very first time at the Blessing ceremony itself. Good grief - why would we jump right into a sexual relationship? I don't think that would have been a very good move. For Unificationists, engaging in a sexual relationship is considered as the highest expression of God's love - very rewarding, worth waiting, for and 'no' not just for procreation only! Remember freedom and responsibility go hand in hand and each couple is totally free to enjoy their sexual relationship as an extension of their love.

My wife and I received the Blessing in the year 1992, but it was only in 1998 that we started our family life. Before we lived together, I invited her to visit my family and relatives first, and she flew from Japan to my hometown in the Philippines to meet them. Nowadays, each couple charts their course in the manner that suits their unique situation best.

Attending the Blessing Ceremony is an eternal commitment that makes it a little more than what the standard 'death do us part' vows proclaim. Another difference is that often times (but this again depends on the couple's situation) the wedding ceremony may not be legally binding, but, no matter, for Unificationists, it's a contract with God, spouse, parents, tribes, and all of humanity, vowing to establish a God-centered global family. It is a really big deal to us and in reality the Unification Church's central and most important sacrament! Indeed, it is our only sacrament.

In the case of my wife and myself, after about six years from the day we received the Blessing, we had a legal marriage in Manhattan, New York, and then we had a Catholic Church extravaganza wedding in the Philippines.

Did I also mention that Unificationists are having so much fun at the Blessing Ceremony, contrary to what the media portrays? As for my experience, it wasn't just a good time, but I experienced overwhelming joy, excitement, and gratitude. Let me ask you something: at some point in your life, did you ever passionately belong to a group that you felt bonded with? Perhaps in an organization where you and your fellow members spent so much time together working on a project, or helping each other? Beyond friends, did your comrades or colleagues feel as if they were your brothers or sisters? This bonding is exactly what I experienced at the Blessing. To distill my feelings at that time, I would say I experienced heaven on earth. Another unique aspect to this shared fellowship is that all of us in the same 'blessing group' share the same anniversary. Now that I have experienced the camaraderie of a shared anniversary it seems very lonely to me for a couple to celebrate their anniversary on their own!

When I joined the Unification Movement, I completely disregarded any plan for my own marital life because I was fully committed to serving God, so I let go of personal desire in thinking about what I wanted in a wife. But when I was asked to prepare for the matching, I jumped with joy! I was very excited. She would be a sister in the Unification family that I would want to spend my whole life being a husband to. My wife had told me that she probably would not have gotten married if not for the Unification Church. Before her joining she was contemplating being single her whole life!

Our matching was done in South Korea. I lived in the Philippines, my wife was Japanese and living in Japan, so we were matched by our photographs. Seeing my wife for the first time in person during the Blessing Ceremony in South Korea was very exciting; immediately we felt that we had already known each other for many years. At that time my wife didn't speak English and I didn't speak Japanese, but we managed to get along well for the entire week and although neither of us spoke Korean we had a wonderful tour of Seoul. Through this experience I can attest to the fact that true love really does break down barriers!

If you want to hear more Blessing Ceremony testimonies, I highly recommend that you find a Unificationist couple and ask them about their own experience. Hear it firsthand from them, not from the people who have never been to the Blessing Ceremony themselves.

Of course, just as in society at large, there are those couples who have divorced or become disillusioned with their ideals. Marriage is not an easy road for any couple all the time. For married couples in any faith or even the secular world there is plenty of guidance and counseling nowadays that is available to nurture a couple through the practical realities of marriage - especially one that crisscrosses cultures and geographical areas. If you talk to an older 'blessed' couple that has been married 30 years or longer you might hear them say that finding God in their spouse was one of the keys to lasting commitment.

Most people think of a union between a husband and wife as only an earthly relationship. But for Unificationists, marriage is eternal, a union both on earth and in the spirit world or life after death. Husband, wife, and the whole family will carry their love over into 'heaven'. Can I live comfortably in heaven if a member of my family is in hell? I surely can not. Again, for a detailed explanation of Heaven and Hell read Chapter 1, The Principle of Creation in the Divine Principle book.

More Than A Church: a vision for a troubled world

The Unification Church has undergone the trials and tribulations that befall many new religions who are regarded with fear and misunderstanding at the outset. There have been growth pangs along the way since its inception in Korea in 1954 when the church was a collection of army ration boxes to its beginnings in America in the 1960s with a handful of missionaries. Then, why is it that Unificationists stay in the church? This is because of its unique vision of what the world can be. The Unification Church is not only a church or a religious organization—it is the ignition throttle for a new world wide culture.

Some Unificationists describe the Divine Principle as an ideology, and some call it philosophy. For me, it's more like an ideology, but I also think of the teaching as principles to live by. Whatever the description, we Unificationists have our own unique culture. We call it the "culture of heart" where people "live for the sake of others." We are not perfect, at all, at practicing this, but we have our eyes on the goal!

For me, the central core of the teachings of the Divine Principle is that God is love, and His most essential aspect is heart. God's purpose of creation is joy. That, too is our purpose!

> After this manner therefore pray ye: Our Father which art in heaven, Hallowed be thy name. Thy kingdom come, Thy will be done in earth, as it is in heaven. (Matthew 6:9-10)

120

What would it be like in the kingdom of heaven on earth? The kingdom of heaven resembles an ideal person.

> *"Where does God's kingdom start? It starts from a perfected person, from the center of that one perfected person. When that happens, God will be dwelling within the center of our hearts." (Rev. Sun Myung Moon; Cheon Seong Gyeong 1261)*

In the 1970s in America "Moonies" were sometimes kidnapped as their parents attempted to break their children's faith by hiring deprogrammers. Rev. Moon was imprisoned on a trumped up tax charge and even now while you are reading this book, there are still Unificationists confined by faith breakers, particularly in Japan. Stories of such incidents can be read at www.religiousfreedom.com.

Despite obstacles and setbacks the "Family Federation for World Peace" as we preferred to be called, is a movement with some exciting accomplishments in the fields of the ocean industry, science, art, education and media outreach. Under the Family Federation umbrella are organizations and businesses such as, The Washington Times, Sun Moon University in Korea and various charitable non-profits including The Women's Federation for World Peace, an NGO at the United Nations. The Little Angels Dance troupe and the Korean Folk Ballet - two harbingers of Good Will were also founded by our movement. To learn more about the founders work go to my website: www.discoverdp.info/founders.html.

> *The kingdom of heaven must first be achieved on earth. What this means is that the kingdom of heaven being established in the physical world is prerequisite to estab-*

lishing the kingdom of heaven in the spirit world. Therefore, heaven is not a world found in outer space on the other side of the galaxy, nor is it the by-product of imagination existing only in the human brain. It refers to the substantial kingdom of heaven on earth, which can only be created when you have led a life expressive of true love. (Rev. Sun Myung Moon, The True Owners in Establishing the Kingdom of Peace and Unity in Heaven and on Earth - II; October 14, 2006)

In the future, there will be no more wars. People fought simply to take from others. However, in the unified world established under God's Kingship, everyone will live for the sake of others; therefore, war will no longer be necessary. People will no longer want to take from their neighbors; instead, your neighbors will try to give you so much that you will have to run away from them ... (November 24, 1991)

Surely there are enough sects and schisms in the world today. Our goal might best be summarized by our slogan, "One Family Under God." Working as a senior pastor, I sometimes joke, "that if the kingdom of heaven does get established, I will lose my job because in heaven we do not need a church!"

The Divine Principle Changes Lives

The Divine Principle changes lives. For most of the people who have accepted it and put it into practice, there is no turning back to their old lifestyles. It changed my life, too providing me with a new spark, a deeper faith, and a personal relationship to God. - oh yes, and a beautiful family.

The *Exposition of the Divine Principle* does not mention his name, but for Unificationists, the Reverend Sun Myung Moon is the Messiah that humanity has been waiting for. Together with his wife, Mrs. Hak Ja Han Moon, they stand as the True Parents of humanity offering salvation through the inheritance of God's lineage through the Blessing Ceremony. One unique aspect to the concept of Messiah or True Parents is that a man alone cannot fulfill the Messianic role; there must be a woman who shares equally not only in his status, but in his providential mission and in the yearning to comfort the broken heart of God.

On September 3, 2012 at the age of 92, the Reverend Sun Myung Moon passed into the spiritual world. Many people have asked, "If Reverend Moon indeed is/was the Messiah, then what did he accomplish by being the Messiah?" If we examine the Bible, Jesus gave us a hint as to what the Messiah's legacy will be:

> Howbeit when he, the Spirit of truth, is come, he will guide you into all truth: for he shall not speak of himself; but whatsoever he shall hear, that shall he speak: and he will shew you things to come. He shall glorify me: for he shall receive of mine, and shall shew it unto you. All things that the Father hath are mine: therefore

said I, that he shall take of mine, and shall shew it unto
you.
John 16:13-15

The *Exposition of the Divine Principle* and the thousands
of volumes of speeches of Reverend and Mrs. Sun Myung
Moon are the New Expression of Truth. With these messages, in the year 1992, they proclaimed the new era, the era of
the Completed Testament Age. The Divine Principle is the
original core book, but there are now three other advanced
ones which comprise "Core Teachings" of the Unification
Church.

If you want to hear more about the Divine Principle and
more about the Unification Movement, I recommend hearing it directly from active Unificationists. There are many
local branches in all of the major cities of the United States
and in other countries. Tell them that you read it first from
this book so that they will know what you have learned so
far about the Divine Principle. You can also visit the website, *www.dplife.info*, to read the Divine Principle contents,
watch lecture videos, read articles about how the Divine
Principle guided individuals to live better lives, and to find
your local branch to meet Unificationists and learn more
about the teachings. And let me end here with this hopeful
quote from Revelation 21:4:

"AND GOD SHALL WIPE AWAY ALL TEARS FROM
THEIR EYES; AND THERE SHALL BE NO MORE
DEATH, NEITHER SORROW, NOR CRYING, NEITHER
SHALL THERE BE ANY MORE PAIN: FOR THE
FORMER THINGS ARE PASSED AWAY."

Made in the USA
Middletown, DE
17 February 2020